THE ULTIMATE COOKBOOK
FOR HOCKEY FAMILIES

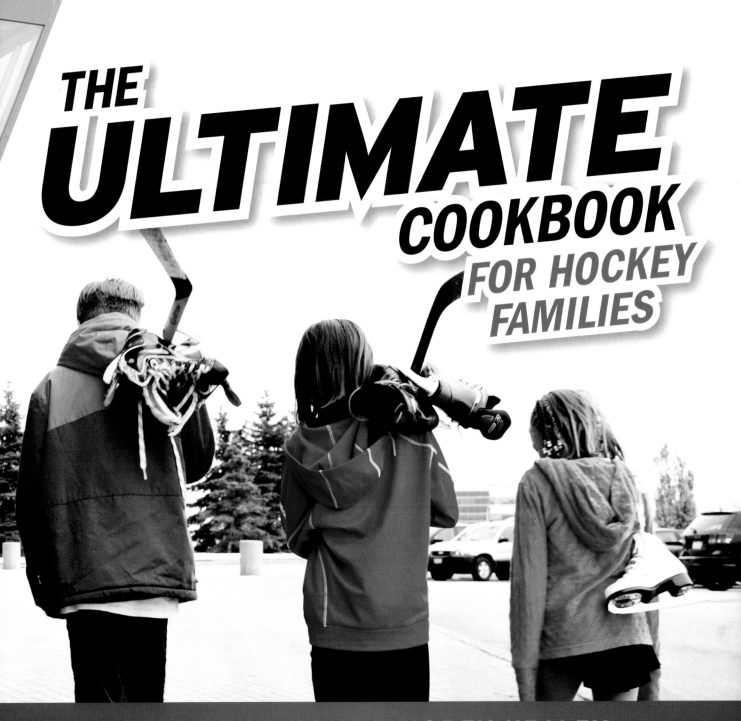

THE ULTIMATE COOKBOOK
FOR HOCKEY FAMILIES

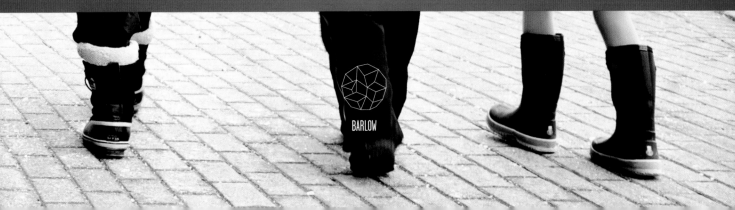

ERIN PHILLIPS AND KOREY KEALEY

BARLOW

Shown on title page (left to right): Alexander, Adam, Rebecca, Ben, Zoë, Niomi.

Progressive PhytoBerry®, Progressive VegeGreens®, and other Progressive products are registered trademarks of the Progressive company and are cited by permission. enerjive Quinoa Skinny Crackers® and other flavours are registered trademarks of enerjive inc. and are cited by permission. Lagostina® is a registered trademark of the Lagostina company and is reproduced by permission.

Library and Archives Canada Cataloguing in Publication data available upon request.

ISBN 978-0-9937656-5-0

Printed in Canada

ORDERS:
In Canada:
  Jaguar Book Group
  100 Armstrong Avenue, Georgetown, ON L7G 5S4

In the U.S.A.:
  Midpoint Book Sales & Distribution
  27 West 20th Street, Suite 1102, New York, NY 10011

Individuals can also buy direct from the authors at **sales@hockeyfood.com**.

SALES REPRESENTATION:
  Canadian Manda Group
  165 Dufferin Street, Toronto, ON M6K 3H6

Cover design: Miriam Blier
Interior design: Kyle Gell Design
Page layout: Kyle Gell Design
Production/Editorial: At Large Editorial Services
Cover and recipe photographs: Valerie Keeler/Valberg Images

For more information, visit **www.barlowbookpublishing.com**

Visit the authors' website at **www.hockeyfood.com**

Barlow Book Publishing Inc.
96 Elm Avenue, Toronto, ON, Canada M4W 1P2

BARLOW

For all of the selfless, supportive parents who never get to stay out late on weekends, who line up early in drive-thru coffee lanes waiting for them to open, who constantly buy new equipment for their ever-growing children, and who always find a way to leave work to drive their kids to early-afternoon practices or Friday tournaments—while simultaneously trying to balance work, school, and the rest of the family. We understand and applaud you, and we hope this book will help to simplify your lives and fuel your families.

CONTENTS

The Pros

A Note from Paul and Stephanie Coffey

As an ex-NHLer and four-time Stanley Cup winner, Paul understands the energy requirements needed for the game of hockey. As parents of two boys playing in the highest level of youth hockey, we focus on nutrition and hydration as much or even more than when Paul played the game. Paul's favourite nutrition advice is to have a big dinner the night before a game and fuel yourself properly the day of the game (this means not overeating). We like to make high-protein energy bars—they're the perfect pre-game snack to eat on the way to the rink!

We are thrilled that Erin and Korey are sharing the advice of those who know the importance of fuel, be it for the game or in life. Play on, kids, and have fun!

Preface

This cookbook has been written for the many dedicated hockey families out there. Early mornings, forgotten equipment, over-zealous fans, "secret" ice, thinking you have shown up on time only to discover the team is already on the ice… Being fully immersed in hockey culture ourselves, we know what it takes to get to the rink.

Today's hectic world often means sports-minded families need to preplan just about everything. This is especially critical when it comes to mealtimes. It can be challenging to supply active children with healthy foods and keep your sanity at the same time. *The Ultimate Cookbook for Hockey Families* can help. This book not only delivers easy-to-understand nutrition advice along with simple recipes and kitchen tips that put it into practice, but it focusses on the foods players need to fuel themselves to achieve optimum performance.

To be honest, what with Erin being a nutritionist, a mom of three, and the wife of longtime Ottawa Senator's defenceman Chris Phillips, and Korey being a recipe developer and mother to three kids who play competitive hockey, we probably didn't need to look much further for inspiration—but we did! We hounded, we begged, and we interviewed pro hockey star wives, mothers, girlfriends, and other hockey-savvy parents for their favourite kitchen recipes, tips, and tricks, and did they ever deliver!

To highlight just a few: Bibbi Alfredsson shares authentic Swedish comfort foods; Sherline Hancock dishes on the broccoli salad that fuelled her daughters Erin (now Phillips) and Kristina to keep up with her and her husband, Barry; and Stephanie Richardson reveals the must-have items for on-the-road and tournament meals.

The Ultimate Cookbook for Hockey Families will give you the equipment to stick handle your way through the grocery aisle and skate around the kitchen with ease, all while avoiding any last-minute penalties at the drive-thru. (Hint: it's not always up to the parents. We show how even the youngest of players can learn and be empowered to make great choices for the love of the game.)

- Part 1, Ultimate Food, provides you with the basics on nutrition—fat, carbs, protein, hydration—and answers the question: how much do you

really need? It also discusses pre- and post-game eating strategies and provides real-life examples direct from the pros.

- Part 2, Ultimate Recipes, provides a full range of breakfast, lunch, snack, and dinner ideas—and, yes, some desserts, too—keeping in mind that busy families don't have a lot of time to spend in the kitchen.

- Throughout the book we present Make Your Own charts (ingredient lists with serving measures that the player can use to customize their own fuel choices), which we think is the best way to get players involved in taking responsibility for their nutrition and building their own menus.

- The Ultimate Appendix contains handy templates for tournament planning and copies of the Make Your Own charts that you can post on the fridge for inspiration or as a reminder of what to pick up at the grocery store. Having the right foods on hand is half the battle.

We hope that players, parents, and family members will enjoy the peak into what some of their favourite players eat and what comfort foods they crave after long road trips away from home. Our ultimate goal, however, is to help simplify your life in the kitchen and empower young players to choose great nutrition, hydration, and recovery and sleep strategies for optimal success in hockey, which will also help them to develop great habits for life.

Erin and Korey

ULTIMATE FOOD: FUEL ADVANTAGE

ULTIMATE FUEL

Hockey is a fast-paced, high-intensity, anaerobic sport. (Anaerobic means your body uses up oxygen more quickly than it can replenish it.) It requires lots of energy, both on and off the ice. And that energy requires fuel.

No matter what level of hockey, players need the right fuel in order to perform to the best of their abilities. Making sure players have the right fuel means paying close attention to what they are eating and drinking at every meal.

While it's true that consuming the proper foods leading up to the big game can make the difference between a lacklustre performance and a phenomenal one, what players eat in the long term, during their off-time, is just as important. Young players are not only developing their hockey skills but also their bodies, brains, and lifelong habits. It's important for players to learn about nutritious options and to develop healthy eating habits. Fortunately, they don't need to rely on a personal trainer or dietitian to do this. They just need to understand a few basics about nutrition.

All of the foods we eat can be divided into three main categories: carbohydrates, protein and fats.

- Our bodies use **carbohydrates** (carbs) to make glucose, which is the fuel that gives us energy. Foods rich in carbohydrates include breads, cereals, grains, fruits, and certain vegetables.

- Every part of our body—cells, tissue, and organs—contains protein, which is constantly being broken down. We need to eat **protein** so our bodies can turn it into amino acids, which are then used to replace the lost proteins. Foods rich in protein include meat, poultry, fish, legumes, eggs, nuts and seeds, dairy, and grains.

- **Fats**—the right kinds of fats (monounsaturated fat and polyunsaturated fat) in the right amounts (see page 25)—are very important to our overall health. They supply calories (energy), help our bodies absorb vitamins, and keep our hearts healthy. Too much of the wrong types of fats (saturated and trans fats) can lead to weight gain and serious health problems.

Carbs, protein, and fats work together to deliver the nutrients we need to fuel our bodies. Players need fuel. The Winning Nutrition diagram below illustrates how much of each type of fuel players need.

WINNING NUTRITION

Coming home with the trophy is what many players dream about. Striving for the win when it comes to good health and nutrition should be every player's goal, too. Fortunately, with a little inspiration, guidance, and determination, that's something every player can attain. For optimum health and sports performance, aim to meet the following recommendations for total daily food and fluid intake.

EVERY DAY:

WATER: 8 CUPS (2 L)

PROTEIN: 10% to 30%

CARBOHYDRATES: 45% to 65%

FATS: 25% to 35%*

* Limit players to no more than 10% saturated fat of their total fat intake per day. For example, based on a daily caloric intake of 1,850 calories per day, a 10-year-old boy should consume no more than 62 g (30%) total fat, including less than 6.2 g saturated fat. A cheeseburger, small fries, and milk contain 10 g of saturated fat—that's far more than his daily requirement in just one meal!

RECOMMENDATIONS FOR TOTAL CALORIE INTAKE PER DAY

Active Children

Females		Males	
ages 4 to 8	1,500 to 1,700 calories	ages 4 to 8	1,650 to 1,850 calories
ages 9 to13	1,700 to 2,250 calories	ages 9 to 13	1,850 to 2,250 calories
ages 14 to 18	2,250 to 2,400 calories	ages 14 to 18	2,250 to 2,800 calories

Based on Canada's Food Guide Recommendations: http://www.hc-sc.gc.ca/fn-an/food-guide-aliment/index-eng.php.

Develop Sound Food and Nutrition Habits

As a professional strength and conditioning coach, I am constantly asked by parents about the best way to enhance their child's sports performance. My answer is to first promote overall good health, which begins with developing sound food and nutrition habits. Here are a few other topics I frequently cover with parents.

Nutritional Knowledge vs. Nutritional Practice

One out of two new athletes I consult with are not getting the proper quality/quantity of fuel necessary to maximize their practices or games. Most athletes know what they need to eat but fail to practise what they know. I find that this frequently occurs because they have developed poor routines and believe that changing these routines requires too much effort. Try to use the tips in this book to significantly change your young athlete's life and diminish the bad habits.

Quality of Sleep

Most athletes are not getting the required 8 to 9 hours of quality sleep they need. This is something that coaches and parents don't emphasize enough. An abundance of research supports the conclusion that without proper sleep, athletes will never reach their potential to learn or to compete. Please ensure your athletes have good sleep habits, which will serve them well throughout their lives.

Simple Routines Before Professional Ones

Parents need to ensure that their athletes are learning and integrating routines that are appropriate for their age/skill level. Often, we try to skip forward and imitate the routines of professional athletes. A good example of this is when athletes stop eating whole foods and start replacing them with a sport supplement because it is convenient and their favourite pro players use it. Don't rush young athletes through the process of becoming a better athlete, and emphasize doing things the right way.

Chris Schwarz
Pro Strength and Conditioning Coach
www.fitquest.ca

CARBOHYDRATES

Carbohydrates are the most important source of fuel for hockey players (or any athlete) because we convert them into energy faster than we can convert protein and fats. Because our bodies are so quick to turn carbohydrates into energy, it's important that we choose healthy sources of carbohydrates (such as Chewy Bar-Downs, page 118, or Foligno's Just-in-Game-Time Pasta Sauce with macaroni, page 231) instead of those that contain excess calories but lack nutrients.

CARBOHYDRATES = ENERGY

SIMPLE VS. COMPLEX CARBS

There are two types of carbohydrates: **simple** and **complex**. Simple carbohydrates are absorbed quickly by our bodies and converted into glycogen, which is how our bodies store glucose for later use. If not used immediately, our bodies convert the glucose into fat. Players should aim to eat simple carbohydrates in moderation. Complex carbohydrates take longer for our bodies to break down, which provide us with fuel for longer periods of time. Players should make total carbohydrates between 45% and 65% of their daily food intake.

Hockey players require both simple and complex carbohydrates. For optimal performance, players should follow these guidelines.

**CONSUME SIMPLE CARBOHYDRATES =
1 HOUR BEFORE PLAY**

**CONSUME COMPLEX CARBOHYDRATES =
3 TO 4 HOURS BEFORE PLAY**

CARBOHYDRATES: TOP CHOICES

Complex Carbohydrates	Total Grams*	Simple Carbohydrates	Total Grams*
black beans (½ cup/125 mL)	20 g	apple (1 medium)	24 g
brown rice (½ cup/125 mL)	23 g	banana (1 medium)	29 g
chickpeas (½ cup/125 mL)	68 g	blackberries (1 cup/250 mL)	14 g
Hockey-Edge Granola (½ cup/125 mL)	44 g	blueberries (1 cup/250 mL)	21 g
multi-grain bagel (half)	28 g	pure maple syrup (1 tbsp/15 mL)	13.5 g
quinoa (½ cup/125 mL)	59 g	orange (1 medium)	21 g
roasted potatoes (½ cup/125 mL)	13 g	orange juice, pure, no sugar added (1 cup/250 mL)	26 g
sweet potatoes (½ cup/125 mL)	22 g	peach (1 medium)	17 g
whole-grain bread (1 slice)	21 g	raw honey (1 tbsp/15 mL)	24 g
whole-grain pasta, cooked (½ cup /125 mL)	21 g	strawberries (1 cup/250 mL)	14 g
		white pasta, cooked (½ cup/125 mL)	18 g
		white rice, short-grain, cooked (½ cup/125 mL)	27 g

Too Much (or Too Little) of a Good Thing

As a general rule, total carbs should make up between 45% and 65% of the daily diet of active children. If we do not eat adequate amounts of carbs, our bodies will turn to stored fats and muscle for energy, which in turn causes our bodies to produce by-products such as lactic acid that can cause cramps or even decrease muscle mass, endurance, and ability. Moderation is key. Eating too many carbs means consuming too many calories. Consuming excess calories can cause obesity, which can have serious health consequences. Whenever possible, follow guidelines on when to select simple over complex carbohydrates.

PROTEIN

Protein plays an instrumental role in building muscle, creating and maintaining a healthy immune system, and maintaining tissue and organ functions. Our bodies turn to our stores of protein as an energy source when glucose (carbs) is not available.

PROTEIN = MUSCLE

As a general rule, to keep their bodies in optimal performance condition, prepubescent kids need about ½ g of protein per 1 lb (0.45 kg) of body weight every day. Very active kids and teens need between ½ and ¾ g of protein per 1 lb (0.45 kg) of body weight every day. For example, a child who weighs 100 pounds (45 kg) needs to consume 50 to 75 g of protein each day.

Meeting these protein requirements is very easy through natural whole food sources; however, protein supplements may be used (see page 70 for tips on boosting protein). Players should consult a sport nutritionist if they have specific concerns about their needs.

Too Much (or Too Little) of a Good Thing

If a player's protein intake is too high, the body will eliminate it through the kidneys or store it as fat. Excess protein can also cause dehydration, a decrease in calcium levels, and kidney problems. If a player's protein intake is too low, the body will begin to break down that hard-earned muscle. Moderation is key.

PROTEIN: TOP CHOICES

	Amount of Protein
almonds (¼ cup/60 mL)	8 g
cheddar cheese (1 oz/30 g)	7 g
chicken, roast (3.5 oz/100 g)	25 g
eggs (1 medium)	6 g
fish fillets (3.5 oz/100 g)	21 g
plain Greek yogurt (½ cup/ 125 mL)	8.4 g
legumes (1 cup/250 mL)	
black beans	15 g
chickpeas	15 g
kidney beans	13 g
milk, 1% (1 cup/250 mL)	9 g
nut butters (1 tbsp/15 mL)	7 g
peanuts (¼ cup/60 mL)	9 g
quinoa (1 cup/250 mL)	8 g
tofu (3.5 oz/100 g)	8 g

FATS

We can't live without fats—literally. But don't confuse body fat and dietary fat (the fats we ingest). There are "good" and "bad" dietary fats. Players need to know the difference. Good fats supply our bodies with essential fatty acids that we are unable to produce on our own. They also help our bodies absorb fat-soluble vitamins. Good dietary fats are crucial in the maintenance of healthy skin, hair, eyes, and brain development. Bad fats clog arteries and increase cholesterol and risk of diseases, such as heart disease and cancer.

BAD FATS VS. GOOD FATS

Saturated fats are found in animal products and by-products and are usually solid at room temperature. (The exception to this rule is coconut oil, which many people now consider a superfood. See page 71 for more information on coconut oil.) **Trans fats** are found in commercially prepared foods and fried foods, usually artificially produced as a result of partial hydrogenation, which is a process used to convert liquids into solids.

BAD FATS = SATURATED AND TRANS FATS

Sources of Saturated Fats:

chicken skin

fatty cuts of beef and pork

fried foods

ice cream

lard

take-out and fast foods

Sources of Trans Fats:

deep-fried or coated foods

frozen dinners

margarine

pancake and waffle mixes

processed and packaged foods (such as hot dogs)

processed cookies, cakes, dough-nuts, and pastries

shortening

GOOD FATS = BRAIN POWER

Good fats, also known as unsaturated fats, include two types of fats: **polyunsaturated fats** and **monounsaturated fats**. When used instead of bad fats, both of these fats can help lower cholesterol and the risk of heart disease. Good fats are also known to protect other organs and support overall health. They help absorb certain vitamins (A, D, E, and K) and facilitate hormone production, brain development, and energy production, all very important to the young player.

Omega-3 fatty acids need to be ingested as the body does not produce them. Great sources include wild salmon, albacore tuna, herring, mackerel, wild trout and anchovies, walnuts, flaxseeds and flaxseed oil, and canola and olive oils. If players aren't consuming enough on a weekly basis, a supplement may be necessary (see page 71).

Fish oil is an excellent source of omega-3 fatty acids. Fish oil supports and strengthens the immune system, helps to control blood sugar levels, and supports brain development. This supplement is also excellent for helping players stay lean during training and competition. The recommended daily dose is 5 mg (see page 71 for tips).

Too Much (or Too Little) of a Good Thing

As a general rule, fats should make up between 25% and 35% of the daily diet of active children, limiting saturated fats to less than 10% and trans fats to less than 1%. Too much good fat will still be stored as fat and may lead to heart disease, obesity, or other chronic conditions. Too little may result in loss of energy, vitamin deficiencies, and many developmental and growth issues.

The best way to keep on top of fat consumption is by looking at food labels. At first, these labels can seem overwhelming, but players can learn how to navigate them quickly. Start by focusing on fats. Look for foods that are low in total fats as well as saturated and trans fats.

GOOD FATS: TOP CHOICES

	Total Grams*
avocado (¼ cup/60 mL)	5.5 g
chia seeds, whole (2 tbsp/30 mL)	
chia seeds	6.4 g
flaxseeds	5 g
coconut oil (1 tbsp/15 mL)	10 g
eggs, omega-3 enriched (1 large)	10 g
fish, cold-water: albacore tuna, herring, wild salmon, mackerel, wild trout, and sardines (4 to 6 oz)	7 to 14 g
raw unsalted nuts (¼ cup/60 mL, or 6 to 10 nuts depending on the size of the hand)	
almonds	7.5 g
cashews	6.5 g
walnuts	9 g
olive oil, cold-pressed extra virgin (1 tbsp/15 mL)	14 g
natural peanut butter (2 tbsp/ 30 mL)	6 g
raw unsalted pumpkin seeds and sunflower seeds (¼ cup/60 mL)	
pumpkin seeds	3 g
sunflower seeds	16 g

ULTIMATE HYDRATION

More than 50% of our body is made up of water, and every internal system we have depends on it. Every day we lose water just by breathing, sweating, and going to the washroom. For our body to function properly, we have to replenish its water supply. Good hydration:

- regulates body temperature
- lubricates joints for flexibility
- strengthens cardiac output (the amount of blood the heart can pump)
- transports nutrients throughout the body for both energy and health
- removes waste like lactic acid, which causes sore muscles

When you think you are thirsty, it is usually too late—your body is already playing catch up and the vital organs that require water are working overtime.

Professional hockey players can lose between 5 and 8 lbs (2 and 3.5 kg) during a game, most of which is fluids (this includes goalies). We mean it when we say that hydration is a key factor in every hockey player's performance. Unfortunately, it's often something most of us forget about in the rush of taking care of other things. Players need to make sure they are are properly hydrated before the puck drops.

Water

Neglecting to maintain proper fluid levels can cause some pretty serious side effects: muscle cramps, dizziness, declining mental function, and fatigue. All of these things will drastically reduce performance during a game (not to mention generally making players feel lousy). So while it's important for players to make sure they are eating the right things at the right times, it's equally important to make sure they are drinking enough all the time.

The recommended daily serving of water is 8 cups (2 L). Follow these suggestions to help break that goal up throughout the day.

- Drink 1 cup (250 mL) of water upon waking up.

- Drink 1 cup (250 mL) of water with each meal.

- Drink 2 cups (500 mL) of water 2 hours before a game or practice. (It usually takes about 40 minutes to fill the bladder, so this will give ample time to make sure players are comfortable for the game and hydrated well enough to perform.)

- Drink 1 cup (250 mL) of water 10 minutes before a game. (Introduce this practice gradually: players shouldn't have to leave the bench during a game or practice to use the restroom.)

- Sip water during all practice and game breaks.

- Drink 1 cup (250 mL) of water 30 to 45 minutes post-workout.

- Drink 1 to 2 cups (250 to 500 mL) of water 45 minutes before bed.

Sports Drinks

While we strongly encourage water as the main source of hydration for a player, sports drinks may be used in cases of extended game schedules (e.g., back-to-back tournament games or 2-hour practices/training camps). Sports drinks aim to replenish fluids and electrolytes (sodium, potassium, and sometimes magnesium) that are lost through sweating during intense workouts (extreme performance lasting longer than 60 minutes).

Please be careful when choosing commercial sports drinks, as they can be high in calories (excess calories will turn into body fat and can cause disease) and the following unhealthy additives:

refined sugars—can cause obesity, type 2 diabetes, and cardiovascular disease, and have no nutritional value

sodium—can cause high blood pressure, kidney disease, and headaches

food colouring—can cause hyperactivity in kids and food sensitivities

Always check the serving size on the label carefully. Quite often the nutritional values listed are only for half of the drink (instead of the whole bottle). It is a good idea to drink half and save the rest for later (or dilute with half water), or make a homemade athletic improvement drink (AID) (see page 31).

HOW TO CALCULATE TEASPOONS OF SUGAR

To calculate the teaspoons of sugar in a drink, take the total grams of sugar (found on the nutritional label) and divide it by 4. For example:

34 g sugar ÷ 4 = 8.5 tsp (42.5 mL) sugar

How to Make Your Own AID

Making a homemade athletic improvement drink (AID) is easy—and better for overall performance! Simply combining coconut water (which is the thin liquid inside young, green coconuts) and water offers far fewer calories than commercial sports drinks and no artificial flavours or colours. Players don't need to go shopping for young coconuts; coconut water is readily sold in most superstores.

Coconut water is low in calories, contains natural fat that aids in vitamin absorption, is high in potassium (more than 4 bananas' worth), and is low in sodium. Some people do not like the taste of coconut water (it tastes better chilled), but there are many ways to mask it. Here are our favourites.

Korey's Pom-AID

½ cup (125 mL)	coconut water
1 cup (250 mL)	water
½ cup (125 mL)	pure unsweetened pomegranate juice
pinch	Himalayan salt
½ tsp (2.5 mL)	honey

1. Combine all of the ingredients in an airtight container and shake well. Chill before serving.

NUTRITION STATS   *per 1 cup* (250 mL)

Calories 128;   **Fat** 0.5 g;   **Sodium** 127 mg;   **Carbs** 29 g;   **Protein** 0.6 g;   **Sugar** 0.6 g

Makes: 2 cups (500 mL)

Tip   *These drinks should be made on demand. Once made, try to consume them right away. If that's not possible, refrigerate the remainder in an airtight container for no more than 1 day.*

Erin's Lemon-AID

½ cup (125 mL)	coconut water
1 cup (250 mL)	water
	Juice of ½ fresh lemon (about 2 tbsp/30 mL)
½ tsp (2.5 mL)	agave syrup or honey
pinch	Himalayan salt
pinch	lemon zest

1. Combine all of the ingredients in an airtight container and shake well. Chill before serving.

NUTRITION STATS   *per 1 cup* (250 mL)

Calories 41;   **Fat** 0 g;   **Sodium** 146 mg;   **Carbs** 10 g;   **Protein** 0 g;   **Sugar** 7.2 g

Makes: 2 cups (500 mL)

Tip   *Himalayan sea salt contains 84 minerals that are good for our bodies. It contains macro minerals (such as calcium and chloride) as well as trace minerals (such as iron and zinc), all of which help replenish the body after sweating.*

Go to www.hockeyfood.com for a downloadable copy of this chart.

AID: ATHLETIC IMPROVEMENT DRINK

Earn huge bragging rights by designing your own athletic improvement drink (AID) made from all-natural ingredients. Mixing and matching flavours is half the fun! What will your signature recovery drink be? (P.K. Subban drinks 4 cups/1 L of coconut water on game days.)

Start with ½ cup (125 mL) pure coconut water, then add one ingredient from each column below.

Liquid (1 to 1½ cups/ 250 to 375 mL)	Sodium (½ tsp/2.5 mL)	Sweetener (½ tsp/2.5 mL)	100% pure fruit juice (max ½ cup/125 mL)
Water	Himalayan salt	Pure maple syrup	Watermelon
Herbal tea		Raw honey	Citrus (orange, lemon, or grapefruit)
		Agave syrup	Pineapple
			Apple
			Pomegranate
			Bloo juice

 If players are undergoing a radical loss of electrolytes, they may experience painful cramping. To help avoid this, add ¼ tsp (1 mL) crushed magnesium tablets or powder to their drink.

Chocolate Milk

Chocolate milk has traditionally been given a bad rap for containing too much sugar, but that perception is quickly changing and many athletes are turning to it after their workouts. Not only does it taste great, but it also meets the body's requirements for fluids, carbs, and protein. In fact, chocolate milk is considered one of the best recovery drinks because of its perfect carbohydrate-to-protein ratio.

Chocolate milk contains both whey protein and casein protein. Whey protein is quickly absorbed by the body and delivered to muscle tissue; by contrast, casein protein takes longer to digest, delivering energy for an extended period of time—an ideal balance.

For optimal recovery, players should aim to replenish their stores of carbohydrates and protein within 30 to 45 minutes of exercise (the time during which the body is most ready to use amino acids to repair muscle tissue and carbohydrates to restore muscle glycogen). Since chocolate milk is usually sold in single-serving cartons at most rinks, it is a quick, easy, and tasty choice right after practice or a big game.

1 cup (250 mL) of chocolate milk contains:

calories: 150	carbs: 26 g
fat: 2.5 g	sugars: 24 g
sodium: 175 mL	protein: 7g
potassium: 0 mg	calcium: 20% of RDA, based on a 2,000-calorie diet

ULTIMATE PERFORMANCE

Great performance in hockey can't be attributed to any one thing. Every pro player has specific beliefs, rules, and strategies for preparing and playing his or her best game. But what they do have in common is this: sleep, hydrate, eat, and repeat. Achieving "ultimate" performance requires proper planning on all fronts.

SLEEP

Getting enough sleep is key. Every kid needs at least 8 to 9 hours of sleep every night in order for their bodies to be able to compete, grow, and repair.

HYDRATE

Staying hydrated just before or after a game is not enough. Following the timing outlined in the previous section (see page 27) will ensure that dehydration won't be an issue and will help form great habits for life.

EAT

A meal plan is not complicated or fancy (see page 272), but it does ensure that players have the necessary fuel to reach their potential.

REPEAT

One day at a time isn't enough. Feeling maximum benefits requires a set and consistently followed routine. This is really where the "ultimate" advantage lies!

Game Day:

Sleep

Hydrate

Eat

Repeat

Chris Neil's Game-Day Routine

Chris's game-day routine starts the night before with his very important night-before game-day dinner. It used to always be steak, but now he sometimes has fish instead. After that, he spends a little time stretching.

Game day starts early for Chris—no rest for the weary when you have three kids! They make sure Daddy is up early.

When Chris is home, he likes to take the kids to the school bus, then he heads off to the rink for his pre-game skate.

After practice, Chris eats his pre-game lunch: chicken with penne pasta and sauce, and green salad with a side of ranch dressing. Next, it's home for a nap. When he wakes up, he likes to have some toast and a coffee, then off to the rink he goes. He likes to be 3 hours early—first in line for treatments (e.g., massage, stretching, physio if needed).

Once he is at the rink, Chris likes to get his head in the game by listening to music, stretching, taping his sticks, and playing some soccer.

Then … it's game time!

Cait Neil,
wife of Chris Neil

Chris Phillips's Game-Day Routine

7:00 a.m.	Wake up and help get the kids on the school bus for 7:30 a.m.
7:30 a.m.	Breakfast: ham, cheese, tomato, mushroom, and pepper omelette; coffee
8:00 a.m.	Off to the rink: treatment, warm-up, stretching, and getting ready for game-day skate (tape sticks, if needed)
9:30 a.m.	Meet with team (usually to discuss the power play)
10:15 a.m.	Game-day skate
10:45 a.m.	Snack: protein shake
11:00 a.m.	Stretch and shower
11:30 a.m.	Pre-game meal: salmon, rice or quinoa, broccoli, green salad; lots of water
12:30 p.m.	Return home to relax and unwind (reading, etc.)
2:00 p.m.	Nap (1½ hours)
3:30 p.m.	Kids home from school; drink lots of water
4:00 p.m.	Snack: toast and raspberry jam
4:30 p.m.	Off to the rink—loves to be early and tape more sticks and coffee
5:30 p.m.	Meeting with team (penalty-killing)
6:00 p.m.	Entire team meeting (strategy); warm-up and massage
7:00 p.m.	Game time

Post-game recovery: drink, ride the bike, stretch, and eat post-game meal (usually chicken and pasta)

Sleep and repeat.

SLEEP LIKE A PRO

Sleep is restorative, healing, rejuvenating, and necessary for success in life and in the game of hockey. With hectic game schedules and different time zones on top of intense workouts, the pros recognize the power of sleep for ultimate performance. It's no surprise that most of the pros include a pre-game nap in their routines.

Parents of younger children can manage sleep schedules with a consistent bedtime and wake time, especially during the school year. At this level, ice times are usually reasonable and the physical activity helps with sleeping.

As players hit the bantam level, it gets a little trickier. Often school, sports, and social calendars become increasingly busy, and ice times are later and longer, sometimes ending at 11:00 p.m. on a school night! In addition, the racing adrenalin and need to eat post-workout can be a recipe for exhaustion. This is when players need to sleep like the pros, taking a 10- to 30-minute nap in the late afternoon.

BETTER SLEEP = BETTER PERFORMANCE

1. Create a bedtime routine, such as taking a hot bath or shower and reading before bedtime.

2. Try to make bedtime the same time every night, keeping in mind that players need at least 8 to 9 hours of sleep a day, depending on the person.

3. Limit fluid intake before bedtime. Getting up to use the washroom interrupts sleep and it may be difficult to fall back to sleep.

4. Avoid eating too late. It can disrupt deep sleep while the body is busy digesting.

5. Eliminate all electronic devices (TV, iPad, phones) at least 1 hour before bed. The lights stimulate the mind.

6. Keep pets out of the room. A restless pet can interrupt sleep, and it may be harder to fall asleep again.

7. Keep the room dark and cool for comfortable sleeping.

8. Wake up at around the same time every day. This helps players develop a sleep pattern.

9. If running on a sleep deficit during busy times, add 1 hour of sleep to the player's routine whenever possible.

PRE-GAME EATING

For hockey players, eating a nutritious pre-game meal is a necessity. It provides their bodies with the fuel needed to hit the ice and play hard. The pros plan their meals carefully—it's an important part of their game-day routines—and quite often they become superstitious about not deviating from their routines. For example, Erin's husband, Chris Phillips, ate the exact same meal at the exact same Italian restaurant before every home game for the first 10 years of his professional hockey career. (Thanks, Tony, at Capones!)

GETTING THE TIMING RIGHT

To allow optimal time for foods to supply the body with energy at the right time, players should eat a pre-game meal 3 to 4 hours prior to a game so they have time to digest it (within 2 to 3 hours). If the body does not get enough time to digest a meal, performance could be impaired, making players feel slow, heavy, and tired on the ice.

PRE-GAME MEAL = 3 TO 4 HOURS BEFORE THE GAME

It's important to make sure that the pre-game meal contains complex carbohydrates (such as brown rice or quinoa), which break down into glucose (energy) much easier than proteins and fats (see page 20) and cause a low rise in blood sugar levels, which means sustained energy for the workout ahead. Avoid foods that are only high in simple sugars (such as white rice, fruit juice, or whole fruits), which cause a rapid rise in blood sugar levels followed by a rapid decrease: the sugar "crash." The "crash" can leave players feeling exhausted, unable to skate or even mentally focus. Players feel like they have hit a wall. See page 45 for guidance on how to tailor a nutritious pre-game meal.

PRE-GAME SNACK = 1 HOUR BEFORE GAME

To keep energy levels high, players should eat a light snack 1 hour before a game. Good examples include Banana Backhanders (page 113) or Pucks on a Bench (page 111), along with a glass of water and a handful of nuts. Eating light keeps energy levels up on the ice. Stay away from greasy foods, refined sugars, or any processed foods to avoid that "crash."

Sample Menus

There are endless possibilities for pre-game meals. Here are a couple quick and easy go-to ideas to inspire menu planning.

Pre-Game Breakfast

- ½ Philly's Blue-Line-Cannon Smoothie (page 68; place other half in a frozen Thermos for between games or post-game)
- 1 cup (250 mL) water

PLUS EITHER:

- **Option 1** 2 slices gluten-free multi-grain toast with peanut butter
- **Option 2** 3 quinoa crackers with natural peanut butter and banana slices

Pre-Game Meal

- **Option 1** 1 serving RJ's Gold-Medal Pre-Game Quinoa with Chicken (page 239)
- **Option 2** 1 serving Make Your Own Meal (page 45)

Post-Game Snack

- **Option 1** 1 to 2 cups (250 to 500 mL) Korey's Pom-AID (page 31) and a handful of mixed nuts; water
- **Option 2** 3 quinoa crackers and 2 tbsp (30 mL) natural peanut butter or hummus; water
- **Option 3** half of one Chewy Bar-Down (page 118); 1 cup (250 mL) chocolate milk

Post-Game Meal

- **Option 1** 1 serving Mediterranean Quinoa Bowl (page 247); water
- **Option 2** 3 cups (750 mL) Line-Saver Lentil Soup (page 177) and 2 to 3 quinoa crackers

P.K. with his mom, Maria.

P. K. Subban

Born: Toronto, ON

Played: Montreal

Fact: Pernell Karl "P. K." Subban won the James Norris Memorial Trophy in 2013, and was tied with Kris Letang as the leading scorer among all defencemen. Subban also won a gold medal with Team Canada at the 2014 Winter Olympics.

"I eat my pre-game meal 7 hours before the puck drops. It consists of organic fish, beef, and whatever else runs, swims, and flys. For carbs, I only eat sweet potatoes and, very rarely, brown rice. I like to top everything off with berries and a litre of coconut water."

P.K. Subban

Go to www.hockeyfood.com for a downloadable copy of this chart.

PRE-GAME MEAL

MAKE YOUR OWN!

Over the years, pre-game meals have evolved. Gone are the days of steak, potatoes, gravy, and dessert. Smart players replace these heavy meals with easily digested, low-sugar, light, and lean foods—the fuel needed to keep them in top shape and sustain them through three periods of intense hockey. Pick and choose your favourite components from the table below to create a winning pre-game meal—the difference in performance will be obvious. This is a great tool to ensure that the best fuel is always accessible.

Choose one item from each column below.

Protein (6 oz/175 g)	Carbohydrates (1 to 2 cups/ 250 to 500 mL)	Veggies (Unlimited)	Sauces & Dips (¼ to ½ cup/ 60 to 125 mL)
chicken	brown rice	artichokes	Alfredo sauce
meatballs	white pasta	asparagus	curry sauce
quinoa	multi-grain bread	avocado	Redden's Rippin' Guacamole (page 128)
salmon	quinoa	broccoli	
tilapia	sweet potatoes	carrots	Quick-Hands Hummus (page 123)
tuna		cauliflower	
		celery	meat sauce
		cucumbers	pesto
		lettuce	Heatley's Light the Lamp Salsa (page 131)
		onions	
		red pepper	teriyaki sauce
		tabbouleh	tomato sauce
		tomatoes	Tripping Tzatziki (page 124)
		Winger Green Juice (page 67)	

Free Agent Pre-Game Meals

Compare your pre-game meal with what the pros are eating.

Player	Protein (6 oz/175 g)	Carbohydrates (1 to 2 cups/ 250 to 500 mL)	Vegetables (Unlimited)	Sauces & Dips (¼ to ½ cups/ 60 to 125 mL)
Chris Neil	chicken	penne pasta	green salad	tomato sauce and Big Rig Ranch Dressing (page 149)
Chris Phillips	broiled salmon	brown rice	broccoli and green salad	
Kyle Turris	Italian pan-fried chicken	farfalle pasta	green salad	alfredo sauce
P.K. Subban	grilled chicken	mashed sweet potato	mixed berries	
Rebecca Johnston	chicken	quinoa	mixed veggies	balsamic dressing

POST-GAME EATING

What players eat after the game is as important as what they eat before it. The 30 minutes directly following game time is crucial recovery time (when our bodies best absorb the nutrients needed to repair tissue and muscle). A good post-game meal will:

- replenish fluids
- refuel energy stores
- provide protein to rebuild and repair muscles
- maintain the immune system after intense exercise
- keep the body ready and able for the next practice or game

POST-GAME SNACK = RECOVERY

See the Make Your Own table on page 48 for ideas on how to build a beneficial post-game snack.

GETTING THE TIMING RIGHT

In order to take advantage of this crucial recovery period, prepare a post-game snack ahead of time to bring to the game or practice; otherwise, players may miss the window of opportunity. (Do the math: 15 minutes in dressing room + 10 to 30 minutes to get home = lost opportunity for optimal recovery and performance.)

POST-GAME MEAL = 30 TO 45 MINUTES AFTER WORKOUT

Depending on the timing of the game or practice (early morning vs. late at night), the post-game snack should be followed by another meal or healthy snack.

Go to www.hockeyfood.com for a downloadable copy of this chart.

POST-GAME SNACK

Post-game snacks need to include a good balance of fluids, carbohydrates, and protein to promote the body's optimal recovery.

Choose one item from each column below.

Fluids (1 to 2 cups/250 to 500 mL)	Snack Choices (amounts specified)
water	1 Chewy Bar-Down (page 118)
coconut water	3 quinoa crackers and 2 tbsp (30 mL) hummus or natural peanut butter
sports AID (see pages 30–31)	½ to 1 cup (125 to 250 mL) Penalty-Kill Parfaits (page 89)
soy milk	1 to 2 hard-boiled eggs and ½ cup (125 mL) veggie sticks
chocolate milk (see page 33)	¼ to ½ cup (60 to 125 mL) Rink Mix (page 108)
	1 to 2 Power Pucks (page 114)
	handful of almonds or mixed nuts (2 tbsp/30 mL to ¼ cup/60 mL)

GAME PLAN FOR SUCCESS

Just like winning the big game, eating well depends on planning and execution, but that doesn't have to be difficult. With a little forethought and a well-stocked fridge (see page 55), players can prepare easy, nutritious, well-balanced pre- and post-game meals and snacks on the fly.

SIMPLE WHOLE FOODS = BEST FUEL FOR PERFORMANCE

The trick lies not in cooking every day but rather in having foods prepared and stored in the fridge and freezer in advance so players can quickly assemble nutritious meals. Anyone can assemble yummy ingredients with a little guidance!

All of the recipes in this book have been selected with busy hockey families in mind. They are quick and easy to prepare, can be frozen for future meals, and provide the fuel families need to fit their lifestyles. Here are some other helpful ways to prepare foods in advance to ensure players always have healthy options within reach.

PROTEIN

- Buy club-size packages of lean ground meats, such as beef, chicken, and turkey. Cook with onions, garlic, and your herbs and spices of choice, then cool and divide into 6 to 8 oz (175 to 250 g) portions that can be tossed into sauces, wraps, salads, soups, and Tessa's World Class Chili (see page 226). There are so many possibilities!

- Roast 2 whole chickens at once, then cool, remove all of the meat, and refrigerate in an airtight container for use in sandwiches, wraps, salads, soups, and quinoa bowls (see pages 232–239) during the week.

- On weekends, grill up chicken, sausages, and beef at the same time, then cool, slice, and refrigerate in airtight containers so they're ready to be added to a plate.

- Hard boil a dozen eggs every Sunday, then cool and refrigerate for use in Off-the-Draw Egg Salad (page 157), snacks, and green salads.

- Keep a bowl of unsalted mixed nuts on the counter for quick snacking.

CARBOHYDRATES

- Cook 2 cups (500 mL) quinoa, rice, or barley, then cool and refrigerate in airtight containers (or freeze individual portions in freezer bags).

- Cook two types of pasta noodles, then strain, cool, and refrigerate in airtight containers.

- Store loaves of high-quality gluten-free and whole multi-grain bread in the freezer. Avoid white "whole-wheat" breads—they have very little nutritional value and the body treats them like refined sugars.

- Bake double batches of muffins or Brekkie Biscuits (see page 96). Cool completely, then individually wrap in plastic wrap and freeze.

- Keep quinoa crackers on hand for dipping or to accompany soups.

FRUIT

- Stock freezer with frozen fruits to have at the ready for Sniper Smoothies (see page 60–81).

- Stock fridge crisper with lots of whole fruits, such as apples, oranges, pears, and plums.

- Pre-wash grapes and refrigerate in an airtight container.

- Buy bunches of bananas for use in Banana Backhanders (page 113), Coach's Wheelin' Peanut Butter and Banana Cookies (page 252), and for snacking. As they become too ripe, peel and freeze for future us in Sniper Smoothies (pages 60–81).

VEGGIES

- Wash and chop veggies (think cucumbers, carrots, celery, and broccoli) and store in snack-size airtight bags.

- Wash grape tomatoes and keep in a bowl on the counter for easy access.

- Purchase lots of avocados at varying stages of ripeness (see page 127). As they ripen, use in Redden's Rippin' Guacamole (page 128), Mexican Quinoa Bowl (page 224), and Foligno's Five-Hole Salad (page 160). Be sure to peel and freeze any unused portions to add to Sniper Smoothies (pages 60–81).

- Have washed and shredded lettuce for quick addition to quinoa bowls (pages 232–239), salads, and wraps.

Food Battles

At some point, each and every professional hockey player was in the same shoes as your player: just a regular kid playing a sport they loved. And their moms and dads were feeding them as best they could—and having the same battles over food, too.

Power struggles over food can be the most unpleasant experiences … especially when they happen three times a day. It may help to understand that there are many reasons why a certain food is unappealing to your player. Sometimes the turn-off can be something as simple as texture (e.g., they hate tomato slices but love tomato sauce).

When your player dislikes something, it is important to get to the root of the issue. Letting them get away with "I don't like it" or "It's gross" doesn't help their nutrition or promote healthy eating habits. Dig a little deeper. Ask what exactly they don't like about that particular food. Get them to be specific.

ASK THE RIGHT QUESTIONS

Temperature Too cold or too hot, not hot or cold enough?

Shape Whole, sliced, rings, wedges—what other way can the food be served?

Size Sometimes size can be overwhelming. Serve in smaller pieces.

Texture Cooked or raw? Peeled or unpeeled? Mashed or whole? Experiment with options.

Colour The same types of fruits and veggies can be available in different colours. Try red peppers if green aren't appealing. Or yellow beans instead of green ones. Peeling removes colour as well!

In short, keep trying, as you never know what you might find out when you dig a little deeper!

KITCHEN ASSIST: THE PLAYER'S PANTRY

Good fuel isn't complicated—and it can actually be rather boring—but with a well-stocked pantry, fridge, and freezer, players can assemble the basics into some fun, deeply nutritious, delicious, and portable meals to help sustain them throughout any day.

Look for natural ingredients—no preservatives—that are low-sodium and low-sugar and that do not contain any trans fats. Real ingredients are key! As they say, if you can't identify what's on the label, you probably shouldn't be putting it in your body.

Here's a list of items we like to keep on hand.

PANTRY

agave syrup

almond milk

avocados (green)

barbecue sauce

beans (black, navy, kidney, garbanzo, etc.), canned

broth, low-sodium

chia seeds, whole

cocoa powder (dark, unsweetened)

coconut water

corn, canned

crackers (enerjive quinoa skinnyQ)

flaxseeds, whole

garlic

honey, raw

lentils, canned

nuts (unsalted raw almonds, cashews, peanuts, and raw walnuts)

olive oil, cold-pressed

onions

potatoes (yellow and sweet)

Progressive PhytoBerry powder

Progressive VegeGreens powder

Progressive OmegEssential powder

Progressive organic coconut oil

rice, brown and white

rice noodles

salsa

seasoning packages (taco, curry, Italian, chili, butter chicken)

soy sauce, reduced-sodium and gluten-free

tomatoes, canned (diced, whole), sauce, paste

vinegars (balsamic, apple cider, red wine)

FRIDGE

apples

asparagus

avocados, ripe (black)

barley (cooked)

beef (cooked)

Bench-Clearing Bean Dip
  (page 132)

berries (blackberries, blueberries,
  raspberries, strawberries)

broccoli

brown rice (cooked)

cabbage

carrots

cauliflower

celery

cheese (cheddar, chevre, feta,
  mozzarella, Parmesan)

chicken (roasted or grilled)

citrus fruit (grapefruit, lemons,
  limes, oranges)

cucumbers

eggs (hard-boiled and raw)

garlic chili paste

ginger root

Greek yogurt (assorted flavours and
  plain)

green onions

Redden's Rippin' Guacamole
  (page 128)

leafy greens (arugula, baby spinach,
  iceberg lettuce, kale, romaine
  lettuce)

maple syrup, 100% pure

Maple Yogurt (page 84)

melons (cantaloupe, honeydew,
  watermelon)

milk

nut butters (almond, cashew, peanut)

bell peppers (red, yellow, green)

pesto

Progressive liquid fish oil

Quick-Hands Hummus (page 123)

quinoa (cooked)

red onion

Heatley's Light the Lamp Salsa
  (page 131)

Tripping Tzatziki (page 124)

Yogurt Cheese (page 126)

zucchini

FREEZER

avocado, peeled and cubed

Bailey's Chicken Sticks (page 167)

banana, peeled

barley, cooked

beef, lean ground

berries (blueberries, raspberries, strawberries)

bread, gluten-free, whole-grain

brown rice, cooked

chicken

fish and seafood (catfish, rainbow trout, salmon, shelled shrimp, tilapia)

frozen mixed vegetables

ice

ice packs

Interference Fish Sticks (page 168)

mango

quinoa, cooked

spinach

ULTIMATE RECIPES: FUEL ADVANTAGE

Sniper Smoothies

Smoothies are one of the easiest, fun, most delicious, and healthy things you can make. Nutrient-dense powerhouse foods that a player may not love on a plate—spinach, avocado, blueberries, and kale, to name a few—can be blended with complementary ingredients to create something that will delight both the player's palate and belly!

Erik Karlsson

Born: Landsbro, Sweden

Played: Ottawa

Fact: After a game, Erik heads straight to the dressing room kitchen to make sure he drinks his recovery smoothie when it'll be most effective.

Karlsson's From-the-Point Berry-Blaster Smoothie

Enhance your power play and blast (shoot) pucks by the goalie from the point (blue line) with ease when you are fuelled like Norris Trophy–winner Erik Karlsson!

Makes: 1 smoothie
Prep: 5 min.
Cook: 0

½ cup (125 mL)	raspberries, fresh or frozen
½ cup (125 mL)	strawberries, fresh or frozen
1	frozen banana, broken into pieces
1 scoop	Progressive PhytoBerry powder
1 scoop	Progressive VegeGreens powder
1 tsp (5 mL)	raw honey (see page 107)
	Water or unsweetened almond milk, to cover

1. In a blender, place ingredients in order listed. Cover and blend on high speed until desired consistency.

MAKE-AHEAD

Freeze individual portions of chopped fruit in resealable bags so you can have a smoothie at the ready any time!

VARIATION

For a banana split smoothie, add 2 tsp (10 mL) dark cocoa powder and 2 tbsp (30 mL) crushed pineapple.

Tip *Consult your doctor or a nutritionist to learn if supplements are right for your player.*

NUTRITION STATS per 1 smoothie

Calories 390; **Fat** 2 g; **Sodium** 30 mg; **Carbs** 94 g; **Fibre** 12 g; **Protein** 4 g

Tip-In Apple-Pie Smoothie

Makes: 1
Prep: 5 min.
Cook: 0

React fast, read the play, and get the stick on the puck to redirect it past the goalie (tip-in) for all the glory. A homey and cozy smoothie that can serve as breakfast, a snack, or even dessert!

1 cup (250 mL)	1% milk or unsweetened almond milk
½ cup (125 mL)	unsweetened applesauce
¼ cup (60 mL)	large-flake rolled oats or quinoa flakes (look for gluten-free)
1 tsp (5 mL)	raw honey
½ tsp (2.5 mL)	ground cinnamon
½ tsp (2.5 mL)	pure vanilla extract
½ cup (125 mL)	ice cubes

1. In a blender, place ingredients in order listed. Cover and blend on high speed until desired consistency.

VARIATION

To make this dairy-free, use unsweetened almond or rice milk.

CINNAMON POWER

Cinnamon assists in regulating blood sugar, so add it to everything! Look for pure cinnamon—sadly, some companies add wheat and other filler ingredients with flavoured cinnamon essence—or grind your own using a spice grinder or kitchen rasp. Read the label and watch out for imposters.

Tip Apples too soft or too bruised for eating? Make your own applesauce. Cut away browned or bruised areas, then peel and chop the rest of the apple. Place pieces in a saucepan with 1 tbsp (15 mL) water per apple. Bring to a boil and simmer for about 15 minutes or until apple is soft. Set aside until cool, then refrigerate in an airtight container.

NUTRITION STATS *per 1 smoothie*

Calories 360; **Fat** 8 g; **Sodium** 120 mg; **Carbs** 58 g; **Fibre** 6 g; **Protein** 15 g

Winger Green Juice

This is an amazing way to get your greens—and their beneficial alkalizing effects—with minimal effort (and without chewing your way through them every day!). With a juicer, the drink is silky smooth. With a high-powered blender, there's only a little more texture and more fibre—the blender is your wingman in the kitchen!

Makes: *3 servings (about 3 cups/750 mL)*
Prep: *15 min.*
Cook: *0*

3 stalks	celery (chopped, if using blender)
2	large kale leaves (stems and centre ribs removed, if using blender)
⅓	English cucumber, unpeeled
large handful	fresh parsley
large handful	fresh spinach
2	green apples (cored, if using blender)
	Juice of 1 lemon
1 inch (2.5 cm)	fresh ginger, peeled (optional)

1. If using a juicer, run ingredients through in order listed. If using a blender, place ingredients in order listed, then cover and blend on high speed until desired consistency.

Tips *To amp up the nutrients in smoothies, use Winger Green Juice instead of water, milk, or other juices.*

Store insulated travel mugs in the freezer to keep drinks cold and slushy longer.

NUTRITION STATS *per 1 cup (250 mL) juice*
Calories 100; **Fat** 1 g; **Sodium** 60 mg; **Carbs** 23 g; **Fibre** 6 g; **Protein** 3 g

Philly's Blue-Line-Cannon Smoothie

Makes: *1 big smoothie*
Prep: *5 min.*
Cook: *0*

This powerhouse of a smoothie will definitely improve the shot (cannon) from the point (blue line). The frozen fruit is a natural sweetener that also makes the smoothie very slushy and delicious.

½ cup (125 mL)	water
½	frozen banana
3 pieces	frozen mango
4	frozen strawberries
½ cup (125 mL)	plain Greek yogurt
1 scoop	Progressive PhytoBerry powder
1 scoop	Progressive VegeGreens powder
1 tsp (5 mL)	Progressive OmegEssential liquid
	Water, to cover

1. In a blender, place ingredients in order listed. Cover and blend on high speed until desired consistency.

VARIATION

For a smoothie that's "pretty and purple" or "brutish and bruised" (depending on who you are talking to), substitute ¼ cup (60 mL) frozen blueberries for the mango.

Tips *Adding the water first prevents powders from clumping or sticking to the blender container.*

Consult your doctor or a nutritionist to learn if supplements are right for your player.

NUTRITION STATS *per 1 smoothie*
Calories 300; **Fat** 4 g; **Sodium** 250 mg; **Carbs** 54 g; **Fibre** 6 g; **Protein** 14 g

Chris with his mom, Carol.

Chris Phillips

Born: Calgary, AB

Played: Ottawa

Fact: Chris loves to have a smoothie after workouts. They're a quick and easy way to meet his nutritional needs as well as a tasty treat that keeps him out of the snack drawer.

Smoothies: Tricks for Boosting Nutrition

What we feed our young players not only helps their bodies develop now, but also establishes a strong foundation for healthy routines that they will carry forward in their lives. Smoothies are fun and easy to make, and we feel that they are the most powerful way to deliver necessary nutrients from vegetables and fruit (especially when fussy eaters come into play).

Sources of Protein

Most players can easily meet protein requirements just by consuming natural whole foods. However, players who are adverse to traditional sources of protein, such as beef, chicken, fish, and nuts, may use protein supplements, especially in smoothies. Consult your doctor or sports nutritionist if you have specific concerns about your player's needs. Try adding one of the following to your smoothies.

- ¼ cup (60 mL) cooked quinoa (adds 2 grams of protein)

- 2 tbsp (30 mL) quinoa flakes (adds 2 grams of protein)

- ¼ cup (60mL) plain Greek yogurt (adds 2 to 3 grams of protein)

- ½ cup (125 mL) 2% milk or almond milk (adds 4 grams of protein)

- Protein powder (follow amount directed on package; we prefer Progressive's Harmonized Protein Cleanest Protein Possible)

Nuts are also a great source of protein and so delicious paired with cocoa, honey, and/or bananas, just to name a few. Add a handful to the blender:

- 2 tbsp (30 mL) almonds (adds 4 grams of protein)

- 2 tbsp (30 mL) chia, flax, or pumpkin seeds (adds 4 grams of protein)

- 2 tbsp (30 mL) sunflower seeds (add 3 grams of protein)

Nut butters are also a great alternative. Just 1 tbsp (15 mL) of nut butter will add about 4 grams of protein, loads of flavour, and a creamy texture to a smoothie (just be mindful of any restrictions related to nut allergies if you plan to take your smoothie to go).

Oils and Supplements

Adding healthy oils and supplements to smoothies provides vital nutrients that players quite likely are not getting enough of from their daily food intake. Consult your doctor or registered nutritionist for guidance on what is best for your player.

Fish oils and omega-3 oils: These oils help to support a developing body and mind, improve focus and concentration, and strengthen the immune system. Look for all-natural ingredients with no sweeteners or preservatives. Choose liquid options whenever possible, as they are absorbed more quickly into the body. (We prefer Progressive's orange-flavoured Ultimate Fish Oil for Kids.) If your player doesn't like the texture, add 1 tsp (5 mL) to a Sniper Smoothie (see pages 60–81)—it's a great way to sneak in these valuable oils (even for adults)!

Coconut oil: Coconut oil used to have a bad reputation for being a saturated fat (a "bad" fat), but we now understand that it is actually a "good" fat (see page 24). Adding 1 tsp (5 mL) coconut oil to your smoothie will increase your good fat intake, give you energy, and can help to strengthen your immune system. Coconut oil is also known to improve cholesterol levels and may even lower your risk of heart disease. When buying coconut oil, look for organic "virgin" coconut oil, which will not be hydrogenated or contain trans fats.

Multivitamins: With the decrease in nutrient quality in many food products and the demanding schedules of kids and parents—not to mention picky eaters and diet restrictions–it can be tough to ensure a player's diet is well rounded and nutritionally sufficient. Giving your player a high-quality children's multivitamin is an easy way to make sure they are getting everything they need. Chewable vitamins can be tossed into smoothies.

Progressive PhytoBerry and VegeGreens powders: Phytoberry powder provides full-body antioxidants, strengthens immunity, and boosts energy and mental clarity (and it tastes yummy, too).VegeGreens contains vitamins and minerals from land, sea, and cruciferous vegetables. It balances PH and strengthens the immune system. Adding just a little to a smoothie provides a lot of extra nutrition.

Centre-Ice Qui'nana Smoothie

We call this one an athlete's dream! Quinoa gives your body a lysine-rich kick that helps with muscle repair. Use a high-powered blender to make this smoothie as smooth as silk.

Makes: 1 smoothie
Prep: 5 min.
Cook: 0

1 cup (250 mL)	unsweetened rice or almond milk
½	frozen banana
¼ cup (60 mL)	cooked quinoa, or more to taste
2 tsp (10 mL)	dark cocoa powder
½ tsp (2.5 mL)	raw honey

1. In a blender, place ingredients in order listed. Cover and blend on high speed until desired consistency.

Tip Freeze ¼ cup (60 mL) portions of cooked quinoa in small resealable bags for grab-and-go protein.

NUTRITION STATS per 1 smoothie

Calories 390; **Fat** 9 g; **Sodium** 220 mg; **Carbs** 67 g; **Fibre** 6 g; **Protein** 14 g

Off-the-Post Purple Smoothie

Makes: 1 smoothie
Prep: 5 min.
Cook: 0

Sometimes that puck hits everything but the net! But when it goes off the post, the adrenalin pumps—and with purple power under your belt, you know the next one's going in! Great purple eye appeal for those hockey players who aren't wild about green drinks.

½ cup (125 mL)	plain Greek yogurt
½ cup (125 mL)	mixed berries, fresh or frozen
½ cup (125 mL)	strawberries, fresh or frozen
¼ cup (60 mL)	chopped purple cabbage
¼	banana, fresh or frozen
1 tbsp (15 mL)	raw honey
	Water, to cover

1. In a blender, place ingredients in order listed. Cover and blend on high speed until desired consistency.

VARIATION

Pour this smoothie into popsicle moulds and freeze to make refreshing purple popsicles.

Tips *For a smoothie that stays cold longer, prepare using mostly frozen ingredients. You may need a little extra liquid for blending frozen fruit.*

Adding purple cabbage and blueberries to your smoothies will camouflage the addition of oh-so-healthy—and oh-so-green—kale, spinach, and avocado, which may be less appealing to young players.

NUTRITION STATS *per 1 smoothie*

Calories 240; **Fat** 1 g; **Sodium** 55 mg; **Carbs** 48 g; **Fibre** 7 g; **Protein** 14 g

Jay with his wife, Lesley.

Jay McClement

Born: Kingston, ON

Played: Toronto, St. Louis, Colorado

Fact: Jay loves to start his day off with this healthy smoothie. It keeps his energy high and contains the necessary nutrients to fuel him through practices and games.

McClement's Penalty-Killing Kale Smoothie

Jay's penalty-killing is no sweat when he's fuelled by high energy and antioxidant-rich superfoods like kale and blueberries. The almond butter in this smoothie adds protein, flavour, and creaminess.

Makes: 1 smoothie
Prep: 5 min.
Cook: 0

1¼ cups (300 mL)	unsweetened almond milk
1 cup (250 mL)	frozen blueberries
2 cups (500 mL)	chopped kale (centre rib removed)
3 tbsp (45 mL)	vanilla Greek yogurt
1 tbsp (15 mL)	almond butter
1 whole	banana, peeled

1. In a blender, place ingredients in order listed. Cover and blend on high speed until desired consistency.

Tip If using plain Greek yogurt, add ½ tsp (2.5 mL) pure vanilla extract and perhaps ½ tsp (2.5 mL) raw honey or pure maple syrup since flavoured yogurt is typically sweeter.

NUTRITION STATS *per 1 smoothie*

Calories 440; **Fat** 13 g; **Sodium** 220 mg; **Carbs** 75 g; **Fibre** 10 g; **Protein** 11 g

Stanley's PB-Cup Smoothie

Makes: 1 smoothie
Prep: 5 min.
Cook: 0

Peanut butter. And chocolate. And banana. This is definitely a smoothie that satisfies—first your taste buds, then your energy needs—possibly even into double overtime of the Stanley Cup Finals!

¼ cup (60 mL)	water
½ cup (125 mL)	plain Greek yogurt
1 tbsp (15 mL)	dark cocoa powder
1 tbsp (15 mL)	natural peanut or almond butter
1	frozen banana

1. In a blender, place ingredients in order listed. Cover and blend on high speed until desired consistency.

VARIATION

For a non-dairy version, omit Greek yogurt and combine ½ cup (125 mL) unsweetened almond or rice milk with ¼ cup (60 mL) quinoa.

Tip Adding the water first prevents powders from clumping or sticking to the blender container.

NUTRITION STATS *per 1 smoothie*
(using natural peanut butter)

Calories 290; **Fat** 9 g; **Sodium** 45 mg; **Carbs** 43 g; **Fibre** 7 g; **Protein** 18 g

Game-Changer Green Smoothie

Makes: 1 smoothie
Prep: 5 min.
Cook: 0

Keep it going deep into the third period as your opponents run out of steam. Games can be changed in seconds, and this green superfuel can help to make the difference! Drink half with breakfast and half as a mid-morning snack.

3	frozen strawberries
1 cup (250 mL)	chopped kale (centre rib removed)
¼	frozen avocado
½	frozen banana
	Juice of 1 lemon
	Water, to cover
1 scoop	Progressive PhytoBerry powder

1. In a blender, place ingredients in order listed. Cover and blend on high speed until desired consistency.

MAKE-AHEAD

Freeze individual portions of chopped fruit in resealable bags so you can have a smoothie at the ready any time!

 **Tips** *Keep an empty stainless-steel Thermos in the freezer. It'll keep your smoothie cold and slushie until you need it later in the day.*

Adding the water first prevents powders from clumping or sticking to the blender container.

Consult your doctor or a nutritionist to learn if supplements are right for your player.

NUTRITION STATS *per 1 smoothie*
Calories 170; **Fat** 5 g; **Sodium** 125 mg; **Carbs** 26 g; **Fibre** 5 g; **Protein** 8 g

SNIPER SMOOTHIE

MAKE YOUR OWN!

Most pro players have a signature smoothie, one that they turn to again and again. Encourage your player to design and name his or her own smoothie. You may be surprised by their selection.

Choose one ingredient from each row below and blend well.						Amount
Base liquid	Water (as much as desired)	Coconut water	Milk	Almond milk	Rice milk		1 cup (250 mL)
Supplemental liquid	Orange juice	Cranberry juice	Pome-granate juice	Bloo juice	Ice (as much as desired)		¼ cup (60 mL)
Fruit	Straw-berries	Blue-berries	Banana or kiwi	Pineapple or mango	Apple or apple-sauce	Avocado (one-quarter)	½ cup (125 mL)
Veggie	Kale (centre rib removed, roughly chopped)	Spinach	Baby carrots	Cucumber	Cooked sweet potatoes or pure pumpkin purée	Wheat grass	1 to 2 cups (250 to 500 mL)
Protein boost	Plain Greek yogurt (½ cup/ 125 mL)	Nut butter (1 tbsp/ 15 mL)	Cooked quinoa (¼ cup/ 60 mL)	Protein powder (as per directions to body weight and age)	Frozen green peas		As specified
Sweetener	Pure maple syrup	Raw honey	Agave syrup				Up to 1 tbsp (15 mL)
Flavouring	Ground cinnamon	Ground nutmeg	Dark cocoa powder	Cocoa nibs	Lime juice	Lemon juice	To taste

2 Breakout Breakfasts

Breakfast really is the most important meal of the day! Think outside the face-off circle for ideas—consider a Brekkie Biscuit (page 96) or Robitaille's Breakaway Burrito (page 103)—and be sure to eat enough to start your day off right. Try to include whole fruit in your meal (instead of fruit juices) or blend it up in a Sniper Smoothie. Just don't skip breakfast!

Maple Yogurt

Makes: *2 cups (500 mL)*
Prep: *5 min.*
Cook: *0*

Adding freshly squeezed lemon juice to regular yogurt causes it to curdle, but Greek yogurt can take it! Sweeten with either pure maple syrup or raw honey to control the sugar content while infusing extreme flavours.

2 cups (500 mL)	plain Greek yogurt
2 tbsp (30 mL)	freshly squeezed lemon juice
2 tbsp (30 mL)	pure maple syrup
1 tsp (5 mL)	ground cinnamon (optional)

1. In a bowl, combine all of the ingredients, adjusting sweetness or tartness to taste. Store in an airtight container in the refrigerator for up to 3 days.

 *Use as a dip for fresh fruit.*

Pair with Hockey-Edge Granola (page 86) and fresh berries.

Use to make Penalty-Kill Parfaits (page 89).

Add to Sniper Smoothies (pages 60–81).

Use as a topping for Break-away Pancakes (page 99).

NUTRITION STATS *per ¾ cup (183 g)*
Calories 130; **Fat** 0 g; **Sodium** 55 mg; **Carbs** 17 g; **Fibre** 0 g; **Protein** 16 g

Greek Yogurt

Greek yogurt is yogurt that has been strained to remove the liquid (whey), resulting in a thicker, creamier texture than regular yogurt. Because it is more concentrated, most brands of Greek yogurt contain almost twice the amount of protein than regular yogurt. Keep rich, thick plain Greek yogurt on hand in the fridge. It's incredibly versatile. You can flavour it to your liking with either sweet or savoury ingredients. Try making the Maple Yogurt (page 84) and serve it on Breakaway Pancakes (page 99) or in Penalty-Kill Parfaits (page 89). Yogurt Cheese (page 126) is very similar to Greek yogurt and easy to make, too!

Hockey-Edge Granola

Makes: 7 to 8 cups (1.75 to 2 L)
Prep: 10 min.
Bake: 20 min.

Homemade gluten-free granola is much cheaper and yummier than store-bought. It also contains a greater amount of protein, a lower amount of refined sugar, and no palm oil—giving athletes the edge on the ice! Invite your players to personalize the fruit and nut selections.

4 cups (1 L)	large-flake rolled oats (look for gluten-free)
1 cup (250 mL)	quinoa flakes
1 cup (250 mL)	raw unsalted pumpkin seeds
½ cup (125 mL)	flaxseeds or chia seeds
¼ cup (60 mL)	chopped walnuts or pecans (optional)
⅓ cup (80 mL)	pure maple syrup or raw honey
3 tbsp (45 mL)	melted coconut oil or vegetable oil
½ cup (125 mL)	mixed dried unsweetened fruit (mango, cranberries, blueberries, raisins, apples, etc.)
2 tbsp (30 mL)	ground cinnamon

Tips *Look for gluten-free oats, which are now available at larger supermarkets.*

Adding the cinnamon and dried fruit while the baked ingredients are still hot keeps the bright cinnamon flavour and the fruit tender and chewy. Also, these ingredients can sometimes burn if included during baking.

Quinoa flakes can be found in most health food stores with the old-fashioned rolled oats.

Make up grab-and-go snacks in small resealable plastic bags.

1. Preheat oven to 350°F (180°C). Lightly grease 2 baking sheets or line with parchment paper.

2. In a large bowl, combine oats, quinoa flakes, pumpkin seeds, flaxseeds, and nuts, if using. Stir in maple syrup and oil.

3. Spread mixture evenly over prepared baking sheets, squeezing bits together to form small clumps. Bake for 15 minutes. Stir mixture, rotate sheets, and bake for 5 minutes more or until granola is golden brown and crunchy.

4. Remove from oven and immediately stir in dried fruit and cinnamon. Cool completely on baking sheets, and then store in an airtight container in the pantry for up to 1 month.

NUTRITION STATS *per ⅓ cup (51 g)*

Calories 220; **Fat** 9 g; **Sodium** 0 mg; **Carbs** 29 g; **Fibre** 5 g; **Protein** 8 g

Chia Seeds

These tiny white and black seeds pack a huge nutritional punch. They are best known for containing omega-3 fats and fibre but also calcium, manganese, and phosphorus. Chia seeds can be eaten whole or ground with the same healthy benefits: boosting energy, stabilizing blood sugar, aiding digestion, and possibly lowering cholesterol, to name a few.

Because chia seeds have hardly any taste, they can be added to everything and anything without changing the flavour. Try them in salads, smoothies, sandwiches, and baked goods. The possibilities are endless.

Try to buy the white and black chia seeds and stay away from the red ones (too young) and the smaller black seeds (known as weeds). You should have no problem finding these at most grocery or health food stores.

Interestingly, chia seeds can absorb nine times their volume in water, providing energy, prolonged hydration, and retention of electrolytes, which is perfect for hockey players.

Penalty-Kill Parfaits

These parfaits are a tournament friend and early morning game-saver! Sometimes players skip nutrient-dense foods when time is tight or there's an early morning game, but that causes energy levels to run low. Those who made a point of being well fuelled are best equipped for penalty-kills.

Makes: 1 parfait
Prep: 5 min.
Cook: 0

¾ cup (175 mL)	Maple Yogurt (page 84)
¾ cup (175 mL)	mixed fresh fruit or ¼ cup (60 mL) dried fruit
¼ cup (60 mL)	Hockey-Edge Granola (page 86)

1. In a vessel of your choice (see Make-Ahead), layer ingredients in the order listed.

MAKE-AHEAD

For eating at home: Have fruit and yogurt ready to go in a covered parfait glass or glass mug in the fridge, and top with granola right before eating.

For eating on the go: Layer everything into a portable cup or glass jar with a tight-fitting lid—and remember to take a spoon!

Tips *Red Solo cups are the perfect disposable vessel when eating on the go.*

If you prefer a reusable container, prepare the parfait in a resealable glass jar (2 cups/500 mL).

Look for extra-long spoons—kids love them and it helps to avoid any mess.

NUTRITION STATS *per 1 parfait* (342 g)
(using fresh strawberries and blueberries)

Calories 340; **Fat** 7 g; **Sodium** 60 mg; **Carbs** 51 g; **Fibre** 6 g; **Protein** 22 g

Tropical Pudding

Makes: 4 to 6 servings
Prep: 10 min.
Cook: 0
Chill: 2 hr.

Easy, creamy, delicious, and dairy-free. Chia-seed protein and fibre provide excellent fuel any time of the day. This is a make-ahead pudding because the chia seeds need time to expand as they absorb the liquids from the fruit. Try other fabulous combinations like strawberry-banana, coconut-cocoa, and blueberry-mango.

1	banana
1 cup (250 mL)	fresh or drained canned pineapple
1½ cups (375 mL)	fresh or frozen mango
1 cup (250 mL)	unsweetened almond milk
¾ cup (175 mL)	chia seeds
	Chopped fruit, such as berries, bananas, coconut (optional)

1. In a food processor, place all of the ingredients in the order listed and process on high speed until smooth. Portion mixture into 4 to 6 resealable 1-cup (250 mL) glass jars. Cover with lid and refrigerate for at least 2 hours or overnight.

2. To serve, remove lid and add chopped fruit, if using.

NUTRITION STATS *per ⅙ recipe* (157 g)
Calories 200; **Fat** 9 g; **Sodium** 35 mg; **Carbs** 26 g; **Fibre** 11 g; **Protein** 6 g

Mel's Pumpkin Gems

Makes: 12 muffins
Prep: 10 min.
Bake: 18 min.

Mel Wilson is that gem of a hockey mom—the one who helps to keep the whole team organized and fed. She has the ability to sneak healthy ingredients into meals without the kids noticing, and these muffins are a perfect example.

1 cup (250 mL)	packed light brown sugar
2	egg whites
1 cup (250 mL)	pure pumpkin purée
¼ cup (60 mL)	melted coconut oil or vegetable oil
⅓ cup (80 mL)	3% vanilla Greek yogurt
¾ cup (175 mL)	quinoa flour
¾ cup (175 mL)	whole-wheat flour
1½ tsp (7.5 mL)	baking powder
1 tsp (5 mL)	ground cinnamon
½ tsp (2.5 mL)	baking soda
½ tsp (2.5 mL)	salt

1. Preheat oven to 350°F (180°C). Line a regular-size muffin pan with paper liners.

2. In a large bowl, whisk together brown sugar and egg whites. Add pumpkin, oil, and yogurt and stir well.

3. In a medium bowl, combine flours, baking powder, cinnamon, baking soda, and salt. Add flour mixture to pumpkin mixture and stir gently just until combined (be careful not to overmix).

4. Scoop batter into muffin cups until three-quarters full. Bake for 18 to 20 minutes or until a toothpick inserted in the centre of a muffin comes out clean. Cool for 5 minutes in the pan, and then turn out onto a wire rack to cool completey. Store in an airtight container for up to 3 days or wrap individually and freeze for up to 3 months.

MAKE-AHEAD
Make a double batch and freeze the extras in an airtight container for up to 3 months.

 **Tips** *Canned pumpkin purée contains protein and beta-carotene and moistens baked goods. Use it to flavour and thicken sauces and soups such as Neil-er's Takedown Vegetable Soup (page 183).*

Freeze leftover pumpkin purée in ice cube trays, transfer portions to a storage container, and add to Sniper Smoothies (pages 60–81).

VARIATIONS

Add ½ cup (125 mL) raisins or dried unsweetened cranberries at the end of step 3 for added fibre, antioxidants, and flavour.

To make gluten-free muffins, substitute amaranth, quinoa, buckwheat, or millet flour for the whole-wheat flour but reduce amount by 2 tbsp (30 mL).

NUTRITION STATS   *per 1 muffin*

Calories 190;   **Fat** 5 g;   **Sodium** 240 mg;   **Carbs** 32 g;   **Fibre** 2 g;   **Protein** 4 g

Coast-to-Coast Hot Cereal

An excellent alternative to pre-packaged, high-sugar, low-fibre instant oatmeal—and it's already packed for cooking! Have your kids' favourite nuts and seeds on hand to throw into the hot cereal. Carrying the puck from end to end (coast to coast) is simple after this complete breakfast!

Serves: 1
Prep: 5 min.
Cook: 0
Stand: 5 min.

¼ cup (60 mL)	large-flake rolled oats (look for gluten-free)
¼ cup (60 mL)	quinoa flakes
2 tbsp (30 mL)	dried unsweetened cranberries
1 tbsp (15 mL)	chia seeds
1 tbsp (15 mL)	pure maple sugar, coconut sugar, or light brown sugar
1 tsp (5 mL)	ground cinnamon
1 cup (250 mL)	boiling water

1. In a heat-proof resealable 2-cup (500 mL) glass jar, combine oats, quinoa flakes, cranberries, chia seeds, sugar, and cinnamon. Seal with lid and store in pantry.

2. To serve, remove lid, add boiling water, stir, cover, and let stand for 5 minutes. Remove lid, stir again, and enjoy.

MAKE-AHEAD

Multiply the dry ingredient measures by 6 for a stockpile of ready-to-go breakfasts.

Tip Avoid sugar crashes from poor hotel-buffet choices while on tournament trips: Remove the coffee basket from the single-serve coffee maker provided in most hotel rooms. Replace the carafe with a resealable glass jar of hot cereal. Then run water through the machine for an easy in-room hot breakfast.

NUTRITION STATS   per 1 recipe (341 g)

Calories 400;   **Fat** 9 g;   **Sodium** 20 mg;   **Carbs** 71 g;   **Fibre** 13 g;   **Protein** 12 g

Brekkie Biscuits

Makes: 12 biscuits
Prep: 15 min.
Bake: 15 min.

Players love the biscuit (puck), so we renamed these savoury ham, egg, and cheddar muffins. Great for grab-and-go breakfasts when your player needs energy for those early morning practices and games. These freeze well, so make extra.

1	onion, finely diced
½ cup (125 mL)	diced red pepper
⅓ cup (80 mL)	diced green pepper
⅓ cup (80 mL)	melted coconut oil or vegetable oil
2 cups (500 mL)	all-purpose flour
¼ cup (60 mL)	ground flaxseeds
1 tsp (5 mL)	baking powder
½ tsp (2.5 mL)	baking soda
1 cup (250 mL)	shredded sharp cheddar cheese
½ cup (125 mL)	diced ham
1	large egg
1¼ cups (300 mL)	milk

1. Preheat oven to 375°F (190°C). Lightly grease a regular-size muffin pan or line with paper liners.

2. In a medium microwave-safe bowl, combine onion, red and green peppers, and oil. Cover and cook on high for 1 to 1½ minutes to soften. Set aside.

3. In a large bowl, combine flour, flaxseeds, baking powder, and baking soda. Stir in cheese and ham.

4. In another bowl, lightly beat egg, and then stir in milk. Add milk mixture and vegetable mixture to dry ingredients. Stir just until moistened.

5. Spoon batter into muffin cups until three-quarters full. Bake for 15 to 18 minutes or until a toothpick inserted in the centre of a muffin comes out clean. Let cool in pan on wire rack for 5 minutes, then turn muffins out to cool completely. Freeze individually wrapped biscuits for up to 3 months.

Tip *Change the veggies to suit the season (asparagus in spring) or your taste buds (jalapeño peppers for a kick), or to use up leftovers (no need to micro-wave—just dice and add grilled or roasted veggies).*

MAKE-AHEAD

For school lunches, pack an individually wrapped frozen biscuit—it'll thaw by noon.

NUTRITION STATS   *per 1 biscuit (100 g)*

Calories 220;   **Fat** 12 g;   **Sodium** 210 mg;   **Carbs** 21 g;   **Fibre** 2 g;   **Protein** 7 g

Berries

Although berries come in different colours, shapes, and sizes, they all have some important things in common: They are low in calories, high in fibre, high in antioxidants, and a good source of vitamins and minerals that our bodies need to function.

Every grocery store carries a wide variety of berries, both fresh and frozen. Check the produce section first. Look for bright, ripe, and firm berries that are free of mould and mildew. Berries taste much better during their peak seasons, and we suggest buying then and freezing them for the winter months. This will not only retain the nutrients but also be much cheaper than buying off-season. Add berries to Make Your Own Sniper Smoothies (page 81) and check out Philly's Blue-Line-Cannon Smoothie (page 68), Karlsson's From-the-Point Berry-Blaster Smoothie (page 63), Penalty-Kill Parfaits (page 89), and Spezza Pie (page 262)!

- **Strawberries:** The most popular berry, strawberries are high in vitamin C (one serving provides up to 150% of the daily recommended vitamin C intake). They are often grown using pesticides, so, if you can, buy organic or, if not available, clean them well just before eating.

- **Blueberries:** Blueberries are high in antioxidants and low on the glycemic index. They, too, are often sprayed with pesticides, so look for organic or wash well.

- **Raspberries:** Raspberries have antioxidant and anti-inflammatory properties. Look for bright-red berries: the riper the raspberries, the more antioxidants they contain.

- **Blackberries:** Blackberries contain vitamin C and bioflavonoids and, compared with other berries, are very low in calories. Look for the darker-coloured berries: a sign that they are high in antioxidants. Blackberries are best consumed raw.

- **Açaí berries:** Grown in South America on açaí palm trees, açaí berries contain antioxidants, fibre, and heart-healthy fats. Most readily available as juice (a great addition to Sniper Smoothies, pages 60–81), you can also find it sold as a supplement in capsules.

Breakaway Pancakes

Makes: 12 to 16 pancakes
Prep: 10 min.
Cook: 5 to 6 min. per batch

Pancakes are a favourite breakfast choice, just not the best pick for long-term energy. But add a few ingredients—like chia seeds to offset carbs with protein, fibre, and omega-3 fatty acids—and switch out syrup for a fruit topping, and pancakes become breakaway fuel for the upcoming game.

1 cup (250 mL)	flour (all-purpose, quinoa, or buckwheat)
1 cup (250 mL)	large-flake rolled oats (look for gluten-free)
¼ cup (60 mL)	ground flaxseed or ground hemp seeds
2 tbsp (30 mL)	chia seeds
1 tsp (5 mL)	baking powder
1 cup (250 mL)	milk or almond milk
2	large eggs, lightly beaten
2 tbsp (30 mL)	melted coconut oil or vegetable oil
1 cup (250 mL)	fresh or frozen berries (optional)

1. In a medium bowl, combine all of the ingredients in order listed (be careful not to overmix).

2. Preheat a non-stick frying pan over medium-high heat and lightly grease.

3. Pour ¼ cup (60 mL) batter per pancake onto hot pan. Cook for 2 to 3 minutes or until edges look dry and bubbles appearing on top begin to pop. Flip and cook for 2 minutes or until golden.

4. Serve with Maple Yogurt (page 84) and additional berries.

MAKE-AHEAD

Double the recipe and freeze the extras. Frozen pancakes can be reheated in the toaster.

Tip For extra protein, top with natural peanut butter or almond butter.

NUTRITION STATS   per 2 pancakes (100 g)

Calories 270; **Fat** 11 g; **Sodium** 110 mg; **Carbs** 34 g; **Fibre** 6 g; **Protein** 10 g

Yorky's Slap Jacks

Makes: 10 slap jacks
Prep: 5 min.
Cook: 2 to 4 min. per batch

From-scratch flapjacks are as quick and easy as boxed versions but without the additives, preservatives, and sodium. The York kids love these pancakes (it's their grandma's recipe), and Jason's wife, Laurel, says it's the only thing Jason makes on his own in the kitchen!

1 cup (250 mL)	all-purpose flour
1 tsp (5 mL)	baking powder
½ tsp (2.5 mL)	salt
1 cup (250 mL)	milk
1	large egg, lightly beaten
½ cup (125 mL)	blueberries, sliced bananas, or raspberries (optional)
2 tbsp (30 mL)	chia seeds (optional)

1. In a medium bowl, whisk together flour, baking powder, and salt. Make a well in the centre of the mixture and add milk and egg. Whisk until smooth. Gently fold in fruit or chia seeds (if using).

2. Preheat a non-stick frying pan over medium-high heat and lightly grease.

3. Pour ¼ cup (60 mL) batter per pancake onto hot pan. Cook for 2 minutes or until edges look dry and air bubbles appearing on top begin to pop. Flip and cook for 1 minute or until golden brown.

4. Serve with fruit, nut butters, or Maple Yogurt (page 84).

MAKE-AHEAD

Take this recipe on the road! Combine the dry ingredients in a large heavy-duty resealable bag. Combine the egg and milk in a resealable glass jar and toss it in your cooler. At mealtime, add the liquid ingredients to the dry, stir well right in the bag, and cook as usual on a griddle.

NUTRITION STATS   *per 2 slap jacks (100 g)*

Calories 190;   **Fat** 7 g;   **Sodium** 690 mg;   **Carbs** 24 g;   **Fibre** 1 g;   **Protein** 6 g

Jason with his wife, Laurel.

Jason York

Born: Nepean, ON

Played: Detroit, Anaheim, Ottawa, Nashville, Boston

Fact: Gramma York's pancakes are a hit with the kids and Jason. In fact, it's one of the few things that Jason will make on his own in the kitchen!

Randy with his sons, Cole and Hunter.

Randy Robitaille

Born: Ottawa, ON

Played: Boston, Nashville, Los Angeles, Pittsburgh, New York, Atlanta, Minnesota, Philadelphia, Lokomotive, Ottawa, Mettallurg, HC Donbass

Fact: Breakfast burritos are quick, easy, nutritious, and travel well. Randy likes to make and bring these to tournaments.

Robitaille's Breakaway Burrito

Having the ability to hustle past defencemen with full control of the puck (breakaway) can redeem and elevate player status, but it requires bursts of speed and intensity. This tasty burrito is a super-easy pre-game meal or after-school snack that's almost foolproof to make in the microwave.

Makes: 1 burrito
Prep: 5 min.
Cook: 30 to 60 sec. in the microwave

1 or 2	large eggs
1	multi-grain flour tortilla (8 inch/20 cm)
2 tbsp (30 mL)	shredded cheddar cheese
2 tbsp (30 mL)	Heatley's Light the Lamp Salsa (page 131) or store-bought
2 tsp (10 mL)	diced green or red onion
1 tbsp (15 mL)	diced avocado or Redden's Rippin' Guacamole (page 128) (optional)

1. In a lightly greased microwave-safe bowl, lightly scramble egg or poke yolk.

2. Cover and microwave on high for 30 to 60 seconds or until cooked. (Time varies with each microwave oven.)

3. Place flour tortilla on a plate. Spread cheese evenly over tortilla. Top with cooked egg, salsa, onion, and avocado (if using). Roll up.

MAKE-AHEAD

For an easy after-school snack, make extra scrambled eggs for breakfast, then roll up a burrito and refrigerate for later. Just reheat on a panini press or in the microwave.

NUTRITION STATS *per 1 burrito* (1 egg) (182 g)

Calories 280; **Fat** 14 g; **Sodium** 850 mg; **Carbs** 23 g; **Fibre** 5 g; **Protein** 14 g

3 Knock-Down Nibbles

Snacks are essential fuel for maintaining long-term energy and help players knock down the hunger that could cause them to eat too much before a game or practice, leaving them sluggish and possibly causing cramps. Include protein at each snack and keep sugar levels relatively low (and always from natural sources). There are a few treats in this chapter: choose when to enjoy them wisely—preferably not on game days!

Play-Review Popcorn

Serves: 1
Prep: 15 min.
Cook: 0

When tournaments are over, reviewing highlights of the games is part of hockey tradition. Coaches will score big with players by serving up a treat like this with the review. Make sure the popcorn is the star with the candy playing a supporting role.

2 cups (500 mL)	unsalted fresh-popped popcorn, cooled slighty
2 tbsp (30 mL)	candy such as gummies or candy-coated chocolate peanuts

1. In a large bowl, combine popcorn and candy.

NUTRITION STATS *per 1 recipe*
(made with air-popped popcorn)

Calories 140; **Fat** 0.5 g; **Sodium** 5 mg; **Carbs** 31 g; **Fibre** 2 g; **Protein** 4 g

Raw Honey

Raw honey is believed to have antibacterial, antifungal, and antiviral properties, so not only is it a delicious natural sweetener, but it can also help to improve overall health. Honey contains vitamin B6, thiamin, riboflavin, pantothenic acid, and niacin. Commercial honey is often overprocessed and may have even been chemically refined, which destroys its beneficial compounds. Be sure to choose "raw" honey, which is unpasteurized and has simply been filtered to help extend its shelf life.

Rink Mix

Makes: 2 cups (500 mL)
Prep: 5 min.
Cook: 0

Better than trail mix! Keep some handy for whenever, wherever you need energy on a moment's notice. In the car … in duffle bags … in purses … and always a big jar of it in the fridge.

6	chocolate quinoa crackers (we prefer enerjive Chocolate FIX Crackers), roughly chopped
¼ cup (60 mL)	roughly chopped raw pecans or walnuts
¼ cup (60 mL)	raw unsalted sunflower seeds
¼ cup (60 mL)	raw unsalted pumpkin seeds
¼ cup (60 mL)	unsweetened coconut flakes
¼ cup (60 mL)	dried unsweetened Goji berries or cranberries
2 tbsp (30 mL)	mini chocolate chips
2 tbsp (30 mL)	toasted hemp seeds

1. In a large bowl, combine all of the ingredients. Transfer to an airtight container and store in the fridge for up to 1 month.

NUTRITION STATS *per 25 g*

Calories 136; **Fat** 9 g; **Sodium** 4.4 mg; **Carbs** 12.6 g; **Fibre** 4.2 g; **Protein** 4 g

Oatmeal

We love rolled oats—they're quick and easy to cook with a variety of ingredients to suit any taste, but we mostly love them for their health benefits: They contain vitamins and minerals (mainly folate, which aids in cell production, and thiamine, which supports muscle and nerve function); they're also a great source of antioxidants, protein, fibre, iron, and complex carbohydrates and can lower your cholesterol levels.

Avoid instant packaged oatmeal, which can contain artificial flavours, preservatives, and too much sodium and sugar. Instead, choose large-flake rolled oats or quick-cooking oats (gluten-free whenever possible) and dress them up with nuts, seeds, fruit (fresh or dried), cinnamon, and pure maple syrup or raw honey. Try them in Hockey-Edge Granola (page 86), Coast-to-Coast Hot Cereal (page 95), Chewy Bar-Downs (page 118), and Winning Apple Crisp (page 265). Rolled oats can also be added to Sniper Smoothies (pages 60–81) for a boost of fibre!

Pucks on a Bench

A hockey version of Bumps on a Log that provides a serving of protein, fruit, and veggie. These score big as a pre-game or post-game snack.

Serves: 1
Prep: 5 min.
Cook: 0

1 stalk	celery, cut in half crosswise
1 tbsp (15 mL)	creamy peanut butter or cream cheese
10	fresh blueberries or raspberries, raisins, or dried unsweetened cranberries

1. Spread ½ tbsp (7.5 mL) peanut butter down centre of each celery piece. Top each with 5 berries.

VARIATION

To make snack school-safe, substitute soy butter, sunflower seed butter, or cream cheese for the peanut butter.

NUTRITION STATS   per 1 recipe
(made with natural, no-salt-added peanut butter)

Calories 100;   **Fat** 8 g;   **Sodium** 35 mg;   **Carbs** 7 g;   **Fibre** 2 g;   **Protein** 4 g

Banana Backhanders

This quick and easily assembled snack came about when Korey's boys (then 5 and 4) went on a fruit-and-veggie strike after staying at a friend's place and snacking on fish crackers, pretzels, chocolate-covered chewy granola bars, and sugar-laden cereals. This got the boys off the picket line and is still a go-to snack 10 years later.

Serves: 1
Prep: 5 min.
Cook: 0

1	banana, sliced into 10 rounds
2 tbsp (30 mL)	creamy peanut butter
5	grapes, sliced in half

1. Arrange banana slices on a plate. Top each slice with a bit of peanut butter and half a grape.

NUTRITION STATS   *per ½ recipe*
(made with natural, no-salt-added peanut butter)

Calories 170;   **Fat** 8 g;   **Sodium** 0 mg;   **Carbs** 24 g;   **Fibre** 3 g;   **Protein** 4 g

Power Pucks

Marketing is everything. Call these "healthy cookies" and 60 percent (or more) of kids won't touch them. Call them Power Pucks and we bet 80 percent of kids at least try them! Sometimes the spin you take when presenting a dish makes it more enticing to your family. This snack is a Phillips family favourite.

½ cup (125 mL)	creamy peanut butter
⅓ cup (75 mL)	raw honey or pure maple syrup
1 tsp (5 mL)	pure vanilla extract
1 cup (250 mL)	large-flake rolled oats (look for gluten-free)
⅔ cup (150 mL)	unsweetened coconut flakes
½ cup (125 mL)	ground flaxseeds or ground chia seeds
1 tbsp (15 mL)	whole chia seeds
¼ cup (60 mL)	chocolate chips, melted

1. In a mixing bowl, using an electric mixer on medium-high speed, cream peanut butter, honey, and vanilla until smooth. Add oats, coconut, flaxseeds, and chia seeds and mix until well combined.

2. Scoop 2 tbsp (30 mL) of mixture and, using your hands, roll it into a ball, then flatten and shape it into a small puck (use a spatula to press and smooth out the puck). Place on a tray. Repeat to make 12 pucks.

3. Smooth ¾ tsp (3 mL) melted chocolate on each puck. Refrigerate for 15 minutes or until chocolate hardens. Store in an airtight container or bag in the fridge for up to 2 weeks or in the freezer for up to 3 months.

Tip To melt chocolate chips in a flash, place in a microwave-safe bowl and heat on Low for 1 minute. Stir, then heat for another 15 to 30 seconds, until chocolate chips are melted. Stir until smooth.

NUTRITION STATS   per 1 puck
(made with natural, no-salt-added peanut butter)

Calories 230;   **Fat** 14 g;   **Sodium** 5 mg;   **Carbs** 25 g;   **Fibre** 6 g;   **Protein** 7 g

Crease-Crasher Cookies

Makes: 36 cookies
Prep: 15 to 20 min.
Bake: 10 min.

Warn the goalie! When this cookie's nutrients get you up to speed, you may not be able to stop quickly! Coconut oil adds antiviral and antibacterial benefits, helps regulate blood sugar, and lowers cholesterol, all of which make this a healthy and tasty cookie to take on tournament.

½ cup (125 mL)	coconut oil or butter, softened
¾ cup (175 mL)	lightly packed light brown sugar
¾ cup (175 mL)	unsweetened applesauce
1	large egg
1 tsp (5 mL)	pure vanilla extract
1 cup (250 mL)	raw unsalted sunflower seeds or pumpkin seeds
½ cup (125 mL)	all-purpose flour
½ cup (125 mL)	whole-wheat flour
½ cup (125 mL)	large-flake rolled oats (look for gluten-free)
⅓ cup (75 mL)	wheat bran
⅓ cup (75 mL)	wheat germ
1 tsp (5 mL)	salt
1 tsp (5 mL)	baking soda
⅓ cup (75 mL)	raisins
⅓ cup (75 mL)	mini chocolate chips

1. Preheat oven to 350°F (180°C). Line 3 baking sheets with parchment paper.

2. In a large bowl, cream together coconut oil and brown sugar. Add applesauce, egg, and vanilla, and stir until light and fluffy.

3. In a medium bowl, combine sunflower seeds, flours, oats, wheat bran, wheat germ, salt, and baking soda. Add dry ingredients to wet ingredients and stir until just combined. Fold in raisins and chocolate chips.

4. Drop 1 tbsp (15 mL) portions of mixture onto prepared baking sheets. Bake for 10 minutes or until golden. Cool on the baking sheet for 5 minutes and then turn out onto a wire rack to cool completely.

5. Store in an airtight container in the fridge for up to 5 days or in the freezer for up to 3 months.

Tip *For a non-dairy cookie, use coconut oil and dairy-free chocolate chips.*

NUTRITION STATS *per 1 cookie*
(using unsweetened applesauce)

Calories 100; **Fat** 6 g; **Sodium** 95 mg; **Carbs** 12 g; **Fibre** 1 g; **Protein** 2 g

Chewy Bar-Downs

Makes: 16 bars
Prep: 15 min.
Bake: 25 min.
Stand: 20 min.

Is a puck hitting the top bar and dropping into the net (bar down) luck or skill? Precision shooting requires mental acuity, patience, and persistent practice. Chia seeds are excellent brain food, supplying omega-3 fatty acids, fibre, and energy. Raw cacao nibs are high in magnesium, fibre, and iron. Put these together and you've got a three-star snack to power practice sessions.

1 cup (250 mL)	creamy peanut butter
2	large eggs
2 tbsp (30 mL)	melted coconut oil or vegetable oil
½ cup (125 mL)	raw honey or agave nectar
2 tsp (10 mL)	pure vanilla extract
2 cups (500 mL)	large-flake rolled oats (look for gluten-free)
1 cup (250 mL)	ground flaxseeds or ground chia seeds
½ cup (125 mL)	quinoa flakes
½ cup (125 mL)	raw cacao nibs or mini chocolate chips
1 cup (250 mL)	crispy rice cereal or rice puffs
2 tbsp (30 mL)	dried unsweetened Goji berries or cranberries (optional)

1. Preheat oven to 350°F (180°C). Line an 8-inch (20 cm) square metal baking pan with parchment paper or waxed paper.

2. In a large bowl, cream together peanut butter, eggs, coconut oil, honey, and vanilla until smooth. Add oats, flaxseed, quinoa flakes, and cacao nibs, and stir until just combined. Fold in crispy rice cereal gently so cereal doesn't get crushed. Stir until just combined.

3. Lightly press mixture into prepared baking pan. Bake for 25 minutes or until firm to touch. Let stand for 20 minutes. Cut into 12 even slices and serve, or store in an airtight container in the fridge for up to 3 days. Freeze in an airtight container or bag for up to 3 months.

NUTRITION STATS *per 1 bar*
(using natural no-salt-added peanut butter)

Calories 315; **Fat** 16 g; **Sodium** 24 mg; **Carbs** 36 g; **Fibre** 6 g; **Protein** 10.5 g

Dip & Chase

Sauces and dips are the perfect way to keep things interesting in the kitchen zone! When you see how easy these are to make yourself, you may not only give up your favourite store-bought brands but also get the player in your house to assist the goal of good nutrition!

Quick-Hands Hummus

Hummus is so easy to make at home, and this very basic recipe is *deelish*. Chickpeas and tahini are both rich in fibre and protein. Chickpeas also contain vitamins and minerals such as folic acid, zinc, and magnesium. If buying pre-made hummus, look for brands that are low in sodium and preservative-free.

Makes: 2 cups (500 mL)
Prep: 10 min.
Cook: 0

1 can (19 oz/540 mL)	chickpeas, rinsed and drained
¼ cup (60 mL)	tahini (sesame paste)
	Finely grated zest and juice of 1 lemon
2 cloves	garlic, finely minced
2 tbsp (30 mL)	extra virgin olive oil
¼ cup (60 mL)	water (or as needed)
	Sprinkle or two of salt and freshly ground black pepper

Garnish (optional)

Drizzle of olive oil
Dash of paprika
Finely chopped fresh parsley leaves

1. Place chickpeas in a food processor or high-speed blender. Add tahini, lemon zest and juice, garlic, and oil. Purée until smooth.

2. With motor running, slowly drizzle in water until mixture reaches a soft, creamy consistency. Taste and season with salt and pepper. Transfer to a bowl and serve immediately, with your garnish of choice, or store in an airtight container in the fridge for up to 5 days.

MAKE-AHEAD

Veggies and dip on the fly! Place 2 tbsp (30 mL) of hummus in the bottom of a resealable 1-cup (250 mL) glass jar. Stand cucumber, carrot, and celery sticks upright in the dip and seal.

Tips *If you don't have tahini on hand, use an equal amount of creamy peanut butter.*

For added protein, add hummus to sandwiches and wraps.

Use as a yummy dip for fresh raw vegetable sticks.

NUTRITION STATS   *per 2 tbsp (30 mL)*

Calories 50; **Fat** 3 g; **Sodium** 45 mg; **Carbs** 5 g; **Fibre** 2 g; **Protein** 2 g

Tripping Tzatziki

Makes: *2 cups (500 mL)*
Prep: *5 min.*
Cook: *0*
Chill: *5 hr.*

A pitch-in-and-help recipe that gets kids measuring, seeding, squeezing, and whirring. And then they can take their homemade snack to school with some quinoa crackers, pita bread, cut-up veggies, or leftover grilled chicken—and plenty of bragging rights!

1½ cups (375 mL)	plain 0% Greek yogurt (no gelatin or starch added)
1 cup (250 mL)	seeded, grated cucumber, squeezed dry
1 clove	garlic, minced
1 tbsp (15 mL)	freshly squeezed lemon juice
	Salt and pepper, to taste
¼ cup (60 mL)	finely chopped fresh dill or 2 tbsp (30 mL) dried dill
1 tbsp (15 mL)	extra virgin olive oil
	2 radishes, grated (optional)

1. In a resealable container, combine all of the ingredients. Cover and refrigerate for at least 5 hours to allow flavours to meld. Store in the fridge for up to 3 days.

Tip *Greek yogurt has double the amount of protein and half the amount of sugar than most other store-bought yogurts.*

NUTRITION STATS *per 2 tbsp (30 mL)*

Calories 20; **Fat** 1 g; **Sodium** 10 mg; **Carbs** 1 g; **Fibre** 0 g; **Protein** 2 g

Yogurt Cheese

Makes: 1½ cups (375 mL)
Prep: 5 min.
Cook: 0
Chill: 2 to 4 hr.

Despite its name, yogurt cheese isn't cheese, but rather a soft, low-fat, cheese-like yogurt spread. It's super easy to make and incredibly versatile. You can control how thick and creamy you like it by adjusting how long you strain it. The only other decision you need to make is how to flavour it—sweet or savoury?

2 cups (500 mL)   plain 2% yogurt (gelatin-free)

1. Line a 6-inch (15 cm) fine-mesh strainer with double layer of cheese-cloth or paper towel. Set over a bowl.

2. Add yogurt to strainer. Cover and refrigerate for 2 to 4 hours to drain. Discard liquid (whey) in bowl. Store yogurt cheese in an airtight container in the fridge for up to 3 days.

VARIATION

Stir in ¼ cup (60 mL) pure maple syrup for a creamy and slightly sweet dip that's perfect on fresh fruit or as a sugar-reduced topping for pancakes.

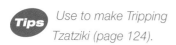 **Tips** *Use to make Tripping Tzatziki (page 124).*

Substitute yogurt cheese for the mayonnaise in dips.

NUTRITION STATS   *per ½ cup (125 mL)*
Calories 130; **Fat** 4 g; **Sodium** 65 mg; **Carbs** 8 g;   **Fibre** 0 g; **Protein** 17 g

Super Avocados

Avocados have recently been recognized as a superfood. They are a rich source of the "good" fat we need—heart-healthy unsaturated fat—as well as fibre. One avocado contains one-third of the recommended daily amount of vitamin C and more than half of the recommended daily amount of vitamin K, which is good for bone growth and maintenance as well as proper cell growth—two things the young hockey player needs!

When grocery shopping, we recommend buying three avocados to have on hand for the week: one that is still green and hard to the touch, one that is both green and brown and firm to the touch, and one that is dark brown and soft to the touch (but not mushy) for immediate use.

Once you get home, store the dark brown one in the fridge for when you want to eat it and leave the other two out on the counter to continue to ripen within a day or two. If you'd like to speed up ripening, set them out close to bananas or, better yet, in a bag with bananas—the ethylene gas produced by bananas causes fruits to ripen more quickly.

Once the avocados are dark brown and soft to the touch, either eat or refrigerate to slow down the ripening process. Only using half? Rub cut avocado with lemon juice to prevent further browning, cover, and refrigerate for up to 1 day.

If your avocados have ripened but you aren't going to use them immediately, you can freeze them! Just halve and peel, and then place on a baking sheet in the freezer until semi-frozen. Transfer to an airtight container and store in the freezer for up to 90 days. They add a creaminess and extra nutrients to Sniper Smoothies (pages 60–81).

Redden's Rippin' Guacamole

Makes: 2 cups (500 mL)
Prep: 5 min.
Cook: 0

The powerhouse nutrients found in avocados, garlic, onion, and lime fuel Wade Redden's rippin' shot on net. Add guacamole to your Mexican Quinoa Bowl (page 246) or Chip-In Chicken Wrap (page 166).

½ cup (125 mL)	minced onion (Vidalia or red)
¼ cup (60 mL)	seeded, minced jalapeño peppers (about 2 peppers)
3	ripe avocados, peeled, pitted, and diced
¼ cup (60 mL)	chopped fresh cilantro leaves
¼ cup (60 mL)	freshly squeezed lime juice (about 2 limes)
2 tsp (10 mL)	minced garlic
1 tsp (5 mL)	sea salt
½ tsp (2.5 mL)	freshly ground black pepper

1. In a medium bowl, combine onion, peppers, and avocados. Mix well. Add cilantro, lime juice, garlic, salt, and pepper and stir thoroughly.

2. Serve with fresh veggies and tortilla chips or quinoa crackers (we prefer enerjive Skinny Quinoa Crackers).

Tip *Create a secret family recipe! Add chili powder, chopped tomatoes, chopped bell peppers, chipotle peppers—there are too many possibilities to list!*

NUTRITION STATS *per ¼ cup (60 mL)*
Calories 80; **Fat** 7 g; **Sodium** 80 mg; **Carbs** 5 g; **Fibre** 3 g; **Protein** 1 g

Wade with his wife, Danica, and kids, Leni and Harper.

Wade Redden

Born: Lloydminster, Saskatchewan

Played: Boston, St. Louis, New York, Ottawa

Fact: The Redden family loves eating this guacamole as an afternoon snack. It's packed with vitamins C, K, B6, and folate and is a great source of fibre, potassium, and healthy fats.

Dany and his girlfriend, Stephanie.

Dany Heatley

Born: West Germany

Played: Anaheim, Atlanta, Ottawa, San Jose, Minnesota

Fact: Dany loves adding this salsa to his meals for a bit of heat and also enjoys it with tortilla chips as a great snack.

Heatley's Light the Lamp Salsa

Everyone is looking for that edge and perfect food regime to "light the lamp" (score a goal and have the red light shine). Adding Heatley's salsa just may give players the heat they need to be a back-to-back 50 goal scorer just like Dany— he actually uses two jalapeños!

Makes: 5 cups (1.25 L)
Prep: 15 min.
Cook: 0
Chill: 2 hr.

1 can (28 oz/796 mL)	no-salt-added diced tomatoes, with juice
2 cups (500 mL)	finely diced tomatoes
¾ cup (175 mL)	finely chopped onion, or to taste
½	jalapeño pepper, seeded and finely chopped
1 clove	garlic, minced
3 tbsp (45 mL)	low-sodium tomato paste (half a small can)
2 tbsp (30 mL)	chopped fresh cilantro leaves
1 tbsp (15 mL)	extra virgin olive oil
2 tbsp (30 mL)	freshly squeezed lime juice

1. In a large bowl, combine all of the ingredients. Cover and refrigerate for at least 2 hours before serving.

VARIATION

To heat it up, add a few dashes of hot sauce or extra jalapeño peppers.

Tips Bring store-bought salsa to life by adding diced fresh tomatoes, lime juice, and/or chopped fresh cilantro leaves.

If you prefer a less-chunky consistency, pulse salsa in a blender. For speed and a finer texture, use an immersion blender. (Kids love to push the buttons!)

NUTRITION STATS *per ¼ cup (60 mL)*
Calories 20; **Fat** 0.5 g; **Sodium** 5 mg; **Carbs** 3 g; **Fibre** 1 g; **Protein** 1 g

Bench-Clearing Bean Dip

Makes: 10 cups (2.5 L)
Prep: 15 min.
Cook: 0

Erin's hockey-playing neighbour Katie Jefferies shared her famous bean dip recipe with us. She's a great role model to Erin's kids, Ben, Zoë, and Niomi, both in the kitchen and on the ice. This make-ahead refrigerator staple tastes even better the next day when flavours have had time to meld and mellow. Tortilla chips are a natural for dipping.

1	red pepper, finely chopped
1	green pepper, finely chopped
4 to 5	green onions, finely chopped
1 can (19 oz/540 mL)	lentils, rinsed and drained
1 can (19 oz/540 mL)	black beans, rinsed and drained
1 can (19 oz/540 mL)	chickpeas, rinsed and drained
1½ cups (375 mL)	reduced-sodium tomato sauce
1½ cups (375 mL)	Heatley's Light the Lamp Salsa (page 131) or your favourite store-bought

1. In a large bowl, combine all of the ingredients. If not serving immediately, cover and refrigerate for up to 5 days.

Tips *Layer in extra flavour and brightness with chopped fresh cilantro leaves and freshly squeezed lime juice, to taste.*

Add to salads, quinoa bowls (see pages 232–239), wraps, and soups for heartier pre-game meals or snacks.

NUTRITION STATS *per ¼ cup (60 mL)*
Calories 40; **Fat** 0.2 g; **Sodium** 125 mg; **Carbs** 7 g; **Fibre** 3 g; **Protein** 2 g

Smash & Scoop Crackers & Dip

This anytime snack is easy to make, fun to eat, and deliciously filling—with practically no cleanup needed. Perfect for after-school snacks or travel food. Be sure to put the avocado in a sturdy container to prevent it from being bruised.

Serves: 4
Prep: 10 min.
Cook: 0

1	avocado, sliced lengthwise and pitted (skin on)
1 tbsp (15 mL)	finely chopped green onions
2 tbsp (30 mL)	sliced grape or cherry tomatoes
2 tbsp (30 mL)	finely chopped cucumber
	Salt and pepper
	Pinch of dried oregano
4 to 6	quinoa crackers (we prefer enerjive Quinoa Skinny Savoury Italian BELLA crackers)

1. Using a fork, mash avocado in the skin. Top each avocado half with green onions, tomatoes, cucumbers, salt and pepper to taste, and oregano.

2. Ditch the fork and scoop with crackers!

Tips *For a great pre-game meal, serve with a grilled chicken breast and ½ cup (125 mL) cooked quinoa.*

If making 1 serving, freeze the other half of the avocado for Sniper Smoothies (see pages 60–81).

NUTRITION STATS *per ¼ recipe*

Calories 130; **Fat** 10 g; **Sodium** 33 mg; **Carbs** 11 g; **Fibre** 9 g; **Protein** 2.5 g

Greens & Toppers

Salads are a superb way to inject vegetables, fibre, and flavour into a player's food regime, but at the same time they can often be the most difficult part of a meal to put together because of the prep work (trying to come up with interesting ways to add variety can be tough, too). Having washed and chopped lettuce ready as well as a yummy dressing is half the battle (and making your own dressing eliminates the preservatives and extra sodium). Try a variety of ingredients and even have your player design their own.

Jason with his wife, Jennifer, and daughters, Nicola and Sophia.

Jason Spezza

Born: Mississauga, ON

Played: Ottawa, Dallas

Fact: You can swap the pears with whatever is in season—berries or apples are terrific, too. Serve with a grilled chicken breast or salmon filet. Jason's wife, Jennifer, loves to pair this with Shoot-Out Sea Bass (page 236). It's a weekly fave at the Spezza table.

PASS (Pear, Almond, & Spinach Salad)

Your family may not pass on the salad when they taste this yummy dressing and pear combination! Jennifer Spezza whips up this great-tasting salad in minutes. Jason loves this with the house specialty, Shoot-out Sea Bass (see page 232).

Serves: 2
Prep: 5 min.
Cook: 0

3 cups (750 mL)	baby spinach leaves
1	pear, thinly sliced
2 tbsp (30 mL)	chopped or sliced blanched almonds

Dressing

2 tbsp (30 mL)	freshly squeezed lemon juice
1 tbsp (15 mL)	extra virgin olive oil
1 tsp (5 mL)	raw honey or pure maple syrup
½ tsp (2.5 mL)	grainy Dijon mustard (optional)
	Salt and pepper

1. Following the order listed, layer salad ingredients in a large serving bowl.

2. In a small bowl, whisk together lemon juice, oil, honey, and mustard (if using). Season with salt and pepper to taste. Drizzle over salad, toss, and serve immediately.

NUTRITION STATS *per ½ recipe*

Calories 190; **Fat** 10 g; **Sodium** 80 mg; **Carbs** 23 g; **Fibre** 4 g; **Protein** 2 g

Clutch Caesar Salad

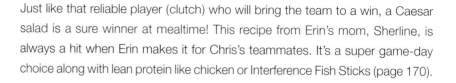

Serves: 4
Prep: 15 min.
Cook: 0

Just like that reliable player (clutch) who will bring the team to a win, a Caesar salad is a sure winner at mealtime! This recipe from Erin's mom, Sherline, is always a hit when Erin makes it for Chris's teammates. It's a super game-day choice along with lean protein like chicken or Interference Fish Sticks (page 170).

4 cups (1 L)	torn romaine lettuce leaves
¼ cup (60 mL)	Clutch Caesar Dressing (page 152)
¼ cup (60 mL)	freshly grated Parmesan cheese
½ cup (125 mL)	baked garlic croutons
¼ cup (60 mL)	chopped cooked bacon (optional)

1. In a large serving bowl, toss together lettuce and dressing. Add cheese and croutons and lightly toss again. Serve immediately.

NUTRITION STATS   *per ¼ recipe* (without bacon)

Calories 120;   **Fat** 7 g;   **Sodium** 170 mg;   **Carbs** 9 g;   **Fibre** 3 g;   **Protein** 4 g

Green Onions

Green onions—also known as scallions or spring onions—are low in calories and can add a lot of flavour to your favourite dishes. They are rich in minerals, phytonutrients, and vitamins, especially vitamins K and C, which are necessary for growth and maintenance of strong bones (if our bodies don't have enough, we'd be much more likely to suffer from bone fractures).

Have green onions on hand (washed and chopped in an airtight container in the fridge) for a quick addition to meals. We love adding them to salads like Roadie's Ham Salad (page 165) and sandwiches like Chip-In Chicken Wrap (page 164), and using them as a garnish for stir-frys, soups like Pho Bucket Soup (page 191), and Quinoa Bowls (pages 232–239).

Tip Try combining 1 cup (250 mL) cooked quinoa, ¼ cup (60 mL) grated carrots, 2 tbsp (30 mL) chopped green onions, 2 tbsp (30 mL) cubed avocado, and 2 tsp (10 mL) reduced-sodium soy sauce—it tastes just like sushi!

Greek Salad

Lettuce-free and hearty, this salad can also be rolled up into a pita with grilled chicken. Serve with Tripping Tzatziki (page 124) on the side.

Serves: 4
Prep: 15 min.
Cook: 0

2 cups (500 mL)	halved grape tomatoes
2 cups (500 mL)	diced cucumber
¼ cup (60 mL)	diced red onion
¼ cup (60 mL)	Balsamic Winger-grette Dressing (page 152)
¼ cup (60 mL)	crumbled feta cheese
2 tbsp (30 mL)	chopped Kalamata olives (optional)

1. In a large serving bowl, toss together tomatoes, cucumber, onion, and dressing. Sprinkle feta cheese and olives (if using) on top. Serve immediately.

NUTRITION STATS *per ¼ recipe*

Calories 130; **Fat** 11 g; **Sodium** 150 mg; **Carbs** 7 g; **Fibre** 1 g; **Protein** 2 g

Muscle Broccoli Salad

This is a power salad if we've ever seen one, full of trophy foods to build muscle and sustainable endurance. It's a favourite of Erin's folks, Barry and Sherline, and it provided the energy Erin and her sister, Kristina, needed to keep up with their uber-athletic parents.

Serves: 4 to 6
Prep: 15 min.
Cook: 0
Chill: 2 hr.

Dressing

¼ cup (60 mL)	0% plain Greek yogurt
2 tbsp (30 mL)	light mayonnaise
1 tsp (5 mL)	pure maple syrup
2 tsp (10 mL)	freshly squeezed lemon juice
	Salt and pepper

Salad

3 cups (750 mL)	broccoli florets
½ cup (125 mL)	sliced red onion
½ cup (125 mL)	raw unsalted sunflower seeds
½ cup (125 mL)	dried unsweetened cranberries
½ cup (125 mL)	crumbled feta cheese

1. In a large bowl, whisk together yogurt, mayonnaise, syrup, lemon juice, and salt and pepper to taste. Cover and refrigerate for at least 2 hours.

2. Remove from fridge. Add broccoli, onion, sunflower seeds, cranberries, and cheese. Stir well. If not serving immediately, salad can be covered and refrigerated for up to 1 day.

Tip Use the leftover broccoli stalks to make Broccoli Shutout Soup (page 184).

NUTRITION STATS *per ⅙ recipe*
(using 0% MF yogurt, light mayonnaise, and dried unsweetened cranberries)

Calories 160; **Fat** 10 g; **Sodium** 160 mg; **Carbs** 13 g; **Fibre** 1 g; **Protein** 6 g

Clutch Caesar Dressing

Makes: *1 cup (250 mL)*
Prep: *10 min.*
Cook: *0*

Garlic is well known as a natural health remedy. Heart-friendly and antimicrobial, it strengthens our immune systems and fights inflammation. It is even known to repel mosquitoes—imagine if it worked on hockey opponents! Erin says this garlicky dressing that her mom, Sherline, made kept the family very healthy.

¼ cup (60 mL)	extra virgin olive oil
¼ cup (60 mL)	red wine vinegar
1 dash	Tabasco sauce
1 dash	Worcestershire sauce
1	large egg yolk or 2 tbsp (30 mL) light mayonnaise
1 tsp (5 mL)	freshly squeezed lemon juice
2 or 3 cloves	garlic, minced
8	capers, drained and chopped
½ cup (125 mL)	freshly grated Parmesan cheese
	Salt and pepper, to taste

1. Place all of the ingredients in a 2-cup (500 mL) resealable wide-mouth glass jar. Using a whisk or immersion blender, or by screwing on the lid and shaking the jar, combine until smooth and creamy. Cover and refrigerate for up to either 2 days (with egg yolk) or 5 days (without egg yolk).

Tip *Don't worry about the raw egg yolk—the lemon juice acts as an acid and "cooks" it.*

NUTRITION STATS *per 1 tbsp (15 mL)*
Calories 50; **Fat** 5 g; **Sodium** 60 mg; **Carbs** 0 g; **Fibre** 0 g; **Protein** 1 g

Big Rig Ranch Dressing

Visit Big Rig restaurant in Ottawa to try this first-hand. Owner Jimmy agreed to let the recipe for the famous dressing out of the bag—for the love of hockey and Chris Phillips. They make it by the gallon, but we scaled it down to family size.

Makes: 1½ cup (375 mL)
Prep: 10 min.
Cook: 0

1 cup (250 mL)	real mayonnaise
¼ cup (60 mL)	sour cream
2 tbsp (30 mL)	buttermilk or plain Greek yogurt
2 tbsp (30 mL)	Dijon mustard
2 tbsp (30 mL)	HP sauce
2 tbsp (30 mL)	granulated sugar
1 tsp (5 mL)	minced garlic
¾ tsp (3 mL)	freshly ground black pepper
¾ tsp (3 mL)	sea salt

1. Place all of the ingredients in a 2-cup (500 mL) resealable wide-mouth glass jar. Using a whisk or immersion blender, or by screwing on the lid and shaking the jar, combine until smooth and creamy. Cover and refrigerate for up to 3 days.

Tips *To reduce total fat: Use lower-fat versions of mayonnaise and sour cream.*

For school lunches, pack dressing in a small container as a dip for fresh veggies.

Use in place of mayonnaise in Roadie's Ham Salad (page 165) and Off-the-Draw Egg Salad (page 159).

NUTRITION STATS *per 1 tbsp* (15 mL)
Calories 70; **Fat** 6 g; **Sodium** 150 mg; **Carbs** 1 g; **Fibre** 0 g; **Protein** 0 g

Balsamic Winger-grette Dressing

Makes: 1 cup (250 mL)
Prep: 5 min.
Cook: 0

Wingers make things happen on the ice, and this dressing does amazing things in the salad bowl! The hint of maple is the subtle secret, but don't limit this only to salads. The dressing is also excellent on pasta, in quinoa and brown rice bowls.

½ cup (125 mL)	extra virgin olive oil
¼ cup (60 mL)	balsamic vinegar
1 tbsp (15 mL)	Dijon mustard
1 tbsp (15 mL)	minced fresh herbs (parsley, chives, and/or basil)
½ tsp (2.5 mL)	pure maple syrup or granulated sugar
	Salt and pepper, to taste

1. Place all of the ingredients in a 1-cup (250 mL) resealable wide-mouth glass jar. Using a whisk or immersion blender, or by screwing on the lid and shaking the jar, combine well. Cover and refrigerate for up to 5 days. Shake before dressing salad.

NUTRITION STATS *per 1 tbsp* (15 mL) *(no salt added)*
Calories 80; **Fat** 8 g; **Sodium** 25 mg; **Carbs** 1 g; **Fibre** 0 g; **Protein** 0 g

Visor-Foggin' Asian Dressing

Garlic, ginger, and rice vinegar lay the Asian flavour base, but the Sriracha and soy sauces are what give a special zing to the dressing and steam up the visor! Use this on noodles, Asian Quinoa Bowl (page 243), grated cabbage, or any green salad.

Makes: $^2/_3$ cup (150 mL)
Prep: 5 min.
Cook: 0

⅓ cup (75 mL)	vegetable oil
⅓ cup (75 mL)	rice vinegar
2 tbsp (30 mL)	reduced-sodium soy sauce (look for gluten-free)
1 tbsp (15 mL)	raw honey or pure maple syrup
1 tbsp (15 mL)	grated fresh ginger
1 clove	garlic, minced
1 tbsp (15 mL)	Sriracha sauce (optional)

1. Place all of the ingredients in a 1-cup (250 mL) resealable wide-mouth glass jar. Using a whisk or immersion blender, or by screwing on the lid and shaking the jar, combine well. Cover and refrigerate for up to 7 days. Shake before dressing salad.

NUTRITION STATS   *per 1 tbsp* (15 mL)

Calories 50;   **Fat** 5 g;   **Sodium** 140 mg;   **Carbs** 2 g;   **Fibre** 0 g;   **Protein** 0 g

6 Lunch Zone

A good lunch is so important for sustaining energy until dinnertime. Trying to whip up something nutritious for lunch early in the morning (as well as keeping storage and food safety in mind) can sometimes feel quite daunting, but the solution is often as easy as assembling a few favourite basics. Depending on the timing, lunches can double as pre-game meals, so it's important to get it right.

Off-the-Draw Egg Salad

Being first to the puck after the face-off (off the draw) requires positioning and speed. Position hard-boiled eggs in the fridge as a speedy lifesaver for ready-made breakfast on the fly. They're also a super snack and lunchtime solution. Try this egg salad atop leafy greens, as a sandwich filling, or with a stack of crackers or veggie sticks for scooping.

Serves: 4
Prep: 10 min.
Cook: 0

4	hard-boiled large eggs, chopped
¼ cup (60 mL)	grated carrots
2 tbsp (30 mL)	finely chopped celery
2 tbsp (30 mL)	minced green onions
2 tbsp (30 mL)	Big Rig Ranch Dressing (page 149) or light mayonnaise

1. In a medium bowl, combine all of the ingredients. Cover and refrigerate for up to 3 days.

NUTRITION STATS   *per 100 g*

Calories 180;   **Fat** 13 g;   **Sodium** 250 mg;   **Carbs** 3 g;   **Fibre** 0 g;   **Protein** 9 g

Eggs

Poached, scrambled, hard-boiled, or coddled, eggs are considered one of the best and most nutritious foods because they contain such a wide variety of nutrients. In the sporting world, eggs are an impressive must: 1 egg yields 6 g of protein, only 77 calories, and is low in fat and carbs. Yet there is much more to eggs than this. They also contain small amounts of almost every mineral and vitamin needed by the body. Remember to eat the yolk as well, as it includes most of the nutrients!

The best way to cook eggs is over low heat to ensure that the lecithin does not break down. Lecithin's main component, choline, helps digest fats, moves wastes and nutrients in and out of cells, and maintains cell permeability. Lecithin, in conjunction with the nervous system, produces acetylcholine, which plays an important role in brain formation, sleep, memory, and learning—all of which are essential to the hockey player! (Try making Off-the-Draw Egg Salad, page 159, as a yummy lunch or snack option.)

How to Make Perfect Hard-Boiled Eggs

Place cold eggs in a single layer in a saucepan. Cover with at least 1 inch of (2.5 cm) cold water. Bring water quickly to a boil over high heat. Immediately cover the saucepan and remove from the heat. Let eggs stand in water, covered, for 15 to 20 minutes for large eggs. Drain water and immediately run cold water over eggs until cooled.

Reach-Back Spinach Salad

Quick and delicious is all-important on hockey nights. Have this salad ready in the fridge and dress it just before serving. The quinoa makes it a complete meal, including protein. Players will reach back for more pucks on the ice and for the salad on the table!

Serves: *4 to 6*
Prep: *15 min.*
Cook: *0*

8 cups (2 L)	baby spinach leaves
2 cups (500 mL)	cooked rice or quinoa
2 cups (500 mL)	bean sprouts
2 stalks	celery, diced
1	green pepper, diced
1 cup (250 mL)	sliced mushrooms
3	green onions, finely chopped
¼ cup (60 mL)	chopped raw unsalted cashews or peanuts

Dressing

½ cup (125 mL)	vegetable oil
¼ cup (60 mL)	reduced-sodium soy sauce (look for gluten-free)
2 cloves	garlic, minced
or	
¾ cup (175 mL)	Visor-Foggin' Asian Dressing (page 153)

1. Following the order listed, layer salad ingredients in a large serving bowl.

2. In a small bowl, whisk together vegetable oil, soy sauce, and garlic. Just before serving, drizzle dressing over salad and toss.

 *Tip* *Sauté leftovers for an amazing stir-fry!*

NUTRITION STATS *per ⅙ recipe*

Calories 310; **Fat** 22 g; **Sodium** 460 mg; **Carbs** 21 g; **Fibre** 4 g; **Protein** 6 g

Foligno's Five-Hole Salad

Serves: 1
Prep: 15 min.
Cook: 0

Heads-up shooting is key for getting the puck between the goalie pads (five-hole). A light, easily digested, nutrient-dense meal keeps the mind sharp and the feet and hands quick. Janelle Foligno calls this winning combination of chicken, avocado, and slow-release complex carbs Nick's perfect pre-game snack.

1	large cooked, cooled chicken breast, diced or shredded
1 tbsp (15 mL)	chopped green onions
1 tbsp (15 mL)	chopped cucumber
2 tbsp (30 mL)	light mayonnaise (more, if needed)
sprinkle	dried thyme
sprinkle	dried dill
pinch	salt and pepper
1	large ripe avocado

1. In a large bowl, combine chicken, green onions, cucumber, mayonnaise, spices, salt, and pepper. Stir well, adding more mayonnaise if needed.

2. Slice avocado lengthwise and remove pit. Place scoop of chicken salad in hole left by pit, letting it overflow a bit.

3. Instead of a spoon, use quinoa crackers (we prefer enerjive Quinoa Skinny Crackers), whole-wheat crackers, or celery sticks for scooping up the salad.

MAKE-AHEAD

Have cooked chicken ready in the fridge or have the entire chicken salad mixed and in the fridge, ready to add to the avocado.

NUTRITION STATS   *per 1 recipe*

Calories 550;   **Fat** 41 g;   **Sodium** 350 mg;   **Carbs** 20 g;   **Fibre** 14 g;   **Protein** 31 g

A young Nick with his mom, Janis.

Nick Foligno

Born: Buffalo, NY

Played: Ottawa, Columbus

Fact: Nick likes to eat this avocado salad bowl when he wakes up from his pre-game nap, before heading to the rink. The protein and healthy fat really help to keep his energy up without leaving him feeling heavy before a game.

Roadie's Ham Salad

Great travel (roadie) food is a must-have for hockey families. We find ham salad a favourite with kids—as a sandwich filling or scoop-up topping for crackers. Look for ham roast that is reduced-sodium, all natural, and without nitrates.

Serves: 3 to 4
Prep: 10 min.
Cook: 0

1 cup (250 mL)	finely chopped ham
½ cup (125 mL)	grated carrots
¼ cup (60 mL)	finely chopped celery
2 tbsp (30 mL)	minced green onions
3 tbsp (45 mL)	Big Rig Ranch Dressing (page 149) or light mayonnaise

1. In a medium bowl, combine all of the ingredients. Cover and refrigerate for up to 3 days.

VARIATION

Make it a melt: Omit the ranch dressing and add ¼ cup (60 mL) shredded cheese. Spread on 4 slices of whole-grain bread and broil on High for 2 to 3 minutes or until cheese is melted and lightly browned.

Tip Use your food processor or high-speed blender to speed up the chopping.

NUTRITION STATS *per ⅓ recipe*

Calories 140; **Fat** 7 g; **Sodium** 650 mg; **Carbs** 8 g; **Fibre** 1 g; **Protein** 10 g

Chip-In Chicken Wrap

Serves: 1
Prep: 5 min.
Cook: 0

Pushing the puck forward and chasing after it ("chip-in") is a great move in hockey. Wraps are a forward move in the nutrition plan. With shredded lettuce, pre-prepped veggies, and cooked meat in the fridge, this is a quick and portable meal. For a crispy, warm option, toss the filled wrap on the panini press or brown it in a pan on the stove top.

1	large multi-grain flour tortilla (10 inches/25 cm)
1 cup (250 mL)	shredded iceberg or romaine lettuce
½ cup (125 mL)	diced or shredded cold, cooked chicken
2 tbsp (30 mL)	Clutch Caesar Dressing (page 146)
1 tbsp (15 mL)	freshly grated Parmesan cheese
1 tbsp (15 mL)	chopped green onions
¼ cup (60 mL)	diced tomatoes (optional)

1. Lay tortilla on clean surface.

2. In a bowl, toss together lettuce, chicken, and dressing. Spread mixture toward the half of the tortilla nearest to you, stopping about 1½ inches (4 cm) from the sides and bottom of the tortilla. Sprinkle with cheese, onions, and tomatoes (if using).

3. Fold each side over mixture. Fold lower portion of tortilla over mixture and side panels, and roll up.

NUTRITION STATS *per 1 wrap*

Calories 430; **Fat** 20 g; **Sodium** 610 mg; **Carbs** 32 g; **Fibre** 6 g; **Protein** 33 g

Jason with his mom, Alicia.

Jason Bailey

Born: Ottawa, ON

Played: Iowa, Binghamton

Fact: Jason likes to eat these crispy chicken sticks (made with chicken breast) once a week as a healthy alternative to fast food.

Bailey's Chicken Sticks

The simplicity of this recipe shows how easy it is to make your own chicken sticks (fingers), and knowing the quality of chicken and breading used gives you peace of mind. Controlling sodium, preservatives, and the amount and type of fat can make the difference in high-level performance.

Serves: 3 to 4
Prep: 15 min.
Bake: 25 min.

2 cups (500 mL)	panko bread crumbs (look for gluten-free)
2	large eggs
	Olive oil or extra virgin coconut oil
1 lb (500 g)	boneless, skinless chicken breast, cut into long strips

1. Preheat oven to 350°F (180°C).

2. Prepare breading station: In a bowl, beat eggs. In a separate shallow dish, place bread crumbs.

3. In a frying pan, over medium-high heat, heat 1 tbsp (15 mL) of oil.

4. Working in batches, dip chicken strips in egg and then bread crumbs, using a fork to press crumbs onto strips. Place in the pan and cook about 2 minutes per side or until crispy. Transfer to a baking sheet. Repeat with remaining chicken. Bake for 20 minutes or until internal temperature reaches 165°F (74°C) on a meat thermometer.

MAKE-AHEAD

Make and freeze big batches for after-school snacks, topping salads, or filling a wrap.

Tips *Chicken Sticks may be prepared and frozen. After baking, refrigerate until cool. Place in an airtight container and freeze for up to 1 month. To serve, remove chicken from the freezer and place on a baking sheet coated with cooking spray. Bake in preheated 400°F (200°C) oven for 15 minutes. Reduce oven to 350°F (180°C) and bake for 10 to 12 minutes more or until crust is golden.*

Use ground quinoa crackers (we prefer enerjive Skinny Quinoa Crackers) as a base instead of panko bread crumbs.

NUTRITION STATS   *per 100 g*

Calories 230;   **Fat** 8 g;   **Sodium** 150 mg;   **Carbs** 2 g;   **Fibre** 0 g;   **Protein** 19 g

Interference Fish Sticks

Serves: 4
Prep: 5 min.
Bake: 18 to 22 min.

Want your kids to eat more fish? Catfish and tilapia are excellent choices because of their mild flavour and meaty texture. Purchase it plain, and season it yourself, or pre-marinated with Cajun spices or lemon pepper to get in the way (interfere) of the kids turning up their noses. Perfect for making fish tacos.

⅓ cup (75 mL)	freshly squeezed lemon juice
2 tbsp (30 mL)	olive oil
¼ cup (60 mL)	freshly grated Parmesan cheese
½ cup (125 mL)	dried bread crumbs (look for gluten-free)
¼ tsp (1 mL)	garlic powder
4	catfish or tilapia fillets, sliced into long strips

1. Position oven rack on the bottom level. Preheat oven to 400°F (200°C). Line a baking sheet with parchment paper or grease thoroughly.

2. Prepare breading station: In a bowl, whisk together lemon juice with oil. In a separate, shallow dish, combine cheese, bread crumbs, and garlic powder.

3. Dip fish in lemon juice mixture and then roll in cheese mixture. Place on prepared baking sheet. Bake for 10 to 12 minutes or until fish is beginning to firm up. Reduce oven to 350°F (180°C) and bake for 8 to 10 minutes more or until coating is golden and fish is cooked through and flakes easily with a fork.

Tip *Fish Sticks may be prepared and frozen. After baking, refrigerate until cool. Place in a freezer-safe container and freeze for up to 1 month. To serve, remove fish from the freezer and place on a baking sheet coated with cooking spray. Bake in preheated 400°F (200°C) oven for 15 minutes. Reduce oven to 350°F (180°C) and bake for 10 to 12 minutes more or until crust is golden.*

NUTRITION STATS *per ¼ recipe*

Calories 320; **Fat** 18 g; **Sodium** 420 mg; **Carbs** 12 g; **Fibre** 0 g; **Protein** 28 g

Praccy Pizza

Make pizza using pita, English muffins, naan, buns, or plain sandwich bread. It is the name and flavour combinations that everyone loves! Let your hockey players design their own pizzas—just ensure there is a fruit or vegetable component either on the pizza or alongside, and pizza is eaten a minimum of 3 to 4 hours before praccy (practice).

Serves: 1
Prep: 10 min.
Bake: 12 to 15 min.

1	small naan bread or pita bread (6 inches/15 cm)
¼ cup (60 mL)	low-sodium tomato sauce
2 tbsp (30 mL)	finely chopped low-sodium nitrate-free ham
2 tbsp (30 mL)	chopped fresh or drained canned pineapple tidbits
2 tbsp (30 mL)	shredded mozzarella cheese

1. Preheat oven to 375°F (190°C).

2. Place naan on a baking sheet. Top with tomato sauce, ham, pineapple, and cheese. Bake for 12 to 15 minutes or until cheese is melted and bread is toasted. Slice and serve.

Tip Keep gluten-free pizza crusts in the freezer for last-minute meal ideas.

NUTRITION STATS *per 1 pizza*
(made with whole-wheat pita (50 g), no-salt-added tomato sauce, and reduced-sodium ham)

Calories 280; **Fat** 8 g; **Sodium** 520 mg; **Carbs** 35 g; **Fibre** 5 g; **Protein** 18 g

How Gluten-Free Eating Will Help Your Hockey Game

Not so many years ago few of us even knew what gluten was let alone how to say it!

Now grocery aisles, blogs, recipes, and entire cookbooks are dedicated to the subject. Celebrity athletes are even endorsing gluten-free eating as a way to up their game by touting benefits from better sleep, better digestion, increased game recovery, and increased mental clarity.

The protein gluten is known to cause abnormal immune function, grain-induced asthma, and inflammation. For an athlete this can result in frequent colds and flus, decreased lung function and oxygen utilization, and increased inflammation. Simply by going gluten-free, a hockey player can experience increased energy, mental clarity, faster recovery time, and decreased inflammation-based injuries.

Here are five easy tips for getting started on a gluten-free lifestyle:

1. Switch the classic spaghetti dinner (wheat pasta) for brown rice pasta or quinoa pasta. For better results, rinse the cooked pasta well.

2. Skip the bread rolls and opt instead for a baked potato or sweet potato.

3. Choose healthy, naturally gluten-free grains such as quinoa, brown rice, or amaranth instead of pasta or bread, and cook them in your rice cooker in vegetable broth for a simple gluten-free side dish.

4. Find a healthy gluten-free bread and swap it for your regular wheat bread. (Look for at least 4 grams of fibre per serving.)

5. View going gluten-free as an opportunity to explore new recipes and foods. Many of the recipes in this cookbook are gluten-free—have fun with them!

Kathy Smart,
North America's gluten-free expert and bestselling cookbook author, nutritionist, and Dr. Oz *guest*

POWER-PLAY LUNCH BOWL

We love this way of assembling our meals. It allows players to make their own lunches and dinners, and provides variety, especially during the week. Just pick an ingredient from each row in the chart below, layer them in a serving bowl, and dig in. (The ingredients shown here are just suggestions— use your imagination and add your favourites!)

Choose one ingredient from each row below and layer in a serving bowl.

Legume, cooked (drained and rinsed if canned) (¼ cup/60 mL)	Chickpeas	Black beans	Kidney beans	Lentils	
Grain, cooked (½ cup/125 mL)	Barley	Quinoa	Rice	Noodles	Bench-Clearing Bean Dip (page 132)
Protein, cooked (4–6 oz/110–175 g)	Chicken	Shellfish	Tofu (firm)	Beef or pork	Shredded cheese 1 oz (30 g)
Leafy greens (unlimited)	Arugula	Spinach	Romaine lettuce	Mesclun mix	Iceberg lettuce
Veggies (unlimited)	Carrots, grated	Green onions, minced	Broccoli florets, fresh or frozen	Peas or corn, fresh or frozen	Sweet peppers (red, yellow, orange, or green), diced
Dressing	Big Rig Ranch (page 149) (1 tbsp/15 mL)	Clutch Caesar (page 146) (1 tbsp/15 mL)	Balsamic Winger-grette (page 150) (1 tbsp/15 mL)	Visor-Foggin' Asian Dressing (page 153) (1 tbsp/15 mL)	Heatley's Light the Lamp Salsa (page 131) (¼ cup/60 mL)
Add-ons	Avocado (one-quarter)	Bacon, crumbled (1 tbsp/15 mL)	Dried unsweetened raisins, blueberries, cranberries (1 tbsp/15 mL)	Pumpkin or sunflower seeds, raw unsalted (2 tbsp/30 mL)	

7 Plus/Minus Soups

Soup is one of the best ways to add vegetables to your player's diet as well as a nutritious way to help keep them hydrated during the day. This chapter contains just a few ideas to get you started. With so many veggies and legumes to choose from, and an assortment of tasty bases—broths and tomatoes and other puréed veggies—you'll discover the options are almost endless. We think soups rank right up there with Sniper Smoothies (pages 60–81) as essential and easy fuel for hockey!

Line-Saver Lentil Soup

This is so delicious, hearty, and easy—perfect fuel for those tight timelines between games during tournaments and training camps. Your linemates will be happy to have you by their side—especially if you fill a couple of thermoses with soup to share.

Serves: 6 to 8
Prep: 15 min.
Cook: 20 min.

1	small onion, minced
2 cloves	garlic, minced
1 stalk	celery, chopped
2	carrots, chopped
1½ cups (375 mL)	chopped smoked ham (nitrate-free)
4 cups (1 L)	cooked or canned reduced-sodium lentils (rinsed and drained if canned)
6 cups (1.5 L)	reduced-sodium chicken broth

1. In a medium saucepan over medium heat, sauté onion, garlic, and celery for 5 minutes or until slightly softened. Add carrots, ham, lentils, and broth. Bring to a boil, reduce heat, and simmer gently, stirring occasionally, for 15 minutes or until carrots are tender. Remove from heat and serve immediately.

VARIATION

For a vegetarian soup, substitute vegetable broth for the chicken broth and omit the ham.

Tip For extra green goodness, add 3 cups (750 mL) baby spinach leaves for the last 3 minutes of cooking.

NUTRITION STATS   *per ⅛ recipe*

Calories 190;   **Fat** 2.5 g;   **Sodium** 320 mg;   **Carbs** 26 g;   **Fibre** 9 g;   **Protein** 17 g

Hold-the-Line Tomato Soup

Serves: *4 to 6*
Prep: *5 min.*
Cook: *15 min.*

By making your own soup, you control the amount of sodium and additives. For cream-based soups, choose 3% plain Greek yogurt instead of traditional cream and milk. That reduces the fat content and adds extra protein and probiotics, along with a tangy zing!

4 cups (1 L)	no-salt-added chicken broth
1 can (28 oz/796 mL)	crushed tomatoes, with juice
	Salt and pepper
1 cup (250 mL)	3% plain Greek yogurt
	Shredded cheddar cheese (optional)
	Croutons (optional)

1. In a medium saucepan over medium heat, combine broth and tomatoes. Bring to a boil, reduce heat, season with salt and pepper to taste, and simmer gently, stirring occasionally, for 15 minutes. Remove from heat.

2. Using an immersion blender, purée soup to desired consistency. Stir in yogurt. Serve immediately, topped with cheese and croutons (if using).

Tips *Using 3% Greek yogurt will ensure that the soup doesn't curdle.*

Make it a meal by ladling soup over ½ cup (125 mL) cooked quinoa and ¼ cup (60 mL) Bench-Clearing Bean Dip (page 132).

NUTRITION STATS *per ⅙ recipe*
(using no-salt-added broth and tomatoes, no cheese or croutons added)

Calories 60; **Fat** 1.5 g; **Sodium** 70 mg; **Carbs** 8 g; **Fibre** 1 g; **Protein** 1 g

Chris with his wife, Caitlin.

Chris Neil

Born: Flesherton, ON

Played: Ottawa

Fact: Chris feels that it's really important to get as much from his food as he can—it helps with performance and his recovery from injury—so this soup loaded with veggies is just the ticket on his days off. It makes a great lunch or starter to accompany dinner.

Neil-er's Takedown Vegetable Soup

Chris Neil is as tough as they come, not to mention quite skilled. It's no wonder he can easily take down any player when he's got this powerful soup in his weekly meal plan! His three kids love it, too.

Serves: 6
Prep: 15 min.
Cook: 15 to 25 min.

2 tbsp (30 mL)	olive oil
3 stalks	celery, chopped
1/2	onion, chopped (or 1 tbsp/15 mL) onion powder)
1	clove garlic, minced
4 cups (1 L)	low-sodium beef broth
1 can (28 oz/796 mL)	diced tomatoes, with juice
1 cup (250 mL)	puréed sweet potato (or peeled, chopped, and cooked sweet potato)
1	head broccoli, about 4 cups (1 L)
1	bay leaf
	Sea salt
pinch	freshly ground black pepper
1 cup (250 mL)	5% light cream

1. In a large saucepan over medium-high heat, heat oil. Sauté celery, onion, and garlic for 5 minutes or until onion is softened. Add beef broth, tomatoes, sweet potato, broccoli, bay leaf, salt to taste, and pepper. Bring to a boil, reduce heat to medium-low, and simmer for 15 minutes or until veggies are fork-tender. Remove from heat. Discard bay leaf.

2. Using an immersion blender, purée soup to desired consistency. Stir in cream. Serve immediately.

NUTRITION STATS *per ⅙ recipe*
(using no-salt-added tomatoes, reduced-sodium beef broth)

Calories 150; **Fat** 8 g; **Sodium** 450 mg; **Carbs** 14 g; **Fibre** 2 g; **Protein** 6 g

Broccoli Shutout Soup

Serves: 8
Prep: 15 min.
Cook: 18 min.

Partway into a game things can sometimes look dismal, but then something turns the game around. The colour of this soup is like that! Not too exciting after boiling, but wait till you add the peas at the end! Green peas are chock full of protein, fibre, and vitamins. So shutout unhealthy alternatives and give this soup a try!

6 cups (1.5 L)	no-salt-added broth (beef, chicken, or vegetable)
4 stalks	celery, chopped
1	head broccoli and stalks, chopped
1	large onion, chopped
2 cloves	garlic, crushed
1 cup (250 mL)	frozen green peas

1. In a large saucepan over medium heat, combine broth, celery, broccoli, onion, and garlic. Bring to a boil, reduce heat, cover, and simmer, stirring occasionally, for 15 minutes or until celery is softened. Remove from heat. Stir in frozen peas.

2. Using an immersion blender, purée until smooth.

Tip *Make it a meal by serving this over ½ cup (125 mL) cooked quinoa and ¼ cup (60 mL) Bench-Clearing Bean Dip (page 132).*

NUTRITION STATS *per ⅛ recipe (using no-salt-added chicken broth)*

Calories 50; **Fat** 0 g; **Sodium** 95 mg; **Carbs** 9 g; **Fibre** 3 g; **Protein** 4 g

Zamboni Soup

The Zamboni is relied on to clean the ice between periods and games in a tournament. This soup can be relied on as part of a perfect pre-game or between-game meal. We always like to have some kind of soup in the fridge, and this sweet potato-leek combination is a winner.

Serves: 4 to 6
Prep: 5 min.
Cook: 30 min.

2 tbsp (30 mL)	vegetable oil
3	large leeks, cut lengthwise, cleaned, and sliced (use only the white and pale-green parts)
1 tsp (5 mL)	dried thyme
1 tsp (5 mL)	dried basil
6 cups (1.5 L)	no-salt-added chicken broth
2	large sweet potatoes, peeled and chopped
¼ cup (60 mL)	chopped fresh parsley leaves (optional)
	Salt and pepper

1. In a large saucepan over medium-high heat, heat oil. Sauté leeks for 1 minute or until slightly softened. Reduce heat to low, cover, and cook for 10 minutes or until leeks are softened and golden but not browned. Stir in thyme, basil, broth, and sweet potatoes. Simmer for 20 minutes or until potatoes are fork-tender. Remove from heat. Add parsley (if using). Season with salt and pepper to taste.

2. Using an immersion blender, purée soup to desired consistency. If too thick, add more broth.

Tips *Make it a meal by serving soup over ½ cup (125 mL) cooked quinoa and ¼ cup (60 mL) Bench-Clearing Bean Dip (page 132).*

If you don't have leeks, use 2 large onions, chopped coarsely.

If you don't have fresh herbs, you can substitute 1 tsp (5 mL) each dried herbs.

NUTRITION STATS **per ⅙ recipe**
(using no-salt-added chicken broth)

Calories 120; **Fat** 4.5 g; **Sodium** 95 mg; **Carbs** 17 g; **Fibre** 2 g; **Protein** 3 g

Grammie Salé's Chicken Soup

Serves: 10
Prep: 15 min.
Cook: about 35 min.

Whenever our young players say their soup is too hot, it's frozen peas (or corn) to the rescue! Adding frozen vegetables at the end lightly cooks them, preserves their colours, and slightly cools the soup for serving. Chickpeas, a great protein and fibre booster, also suppress hunger.

1	large onion, chopped
4	large carrots, diced
5 stalks	celery, diced
1 clove	garlic, minced
3 cups (750 mL)	chopped boneless, skinless chicken breasts or thighs
8 cups (2 L)	no-salt-added chicken broth
2 cups (500 mL)	cooked chickpeas
4 cups (1 L)	cooked whole-wheat spaghettini (or gluten-free noodles)
2 cups (500 mL)	frozen peas
3 tbsp (45 mL)	chopped fresh cilantro leaves or dill

1. In a large saucepan over medium-high heat, sauté onion, carrots, celery, and garlic for 5 minutes or until softened. Add chicken and cook for 8 minutes or until browned and no longer pink in the middle. Stir in broth and chickpeas. Bring to a boil, then reduce heat and simmer for 15 minutes.

2. Add noodles, peas, and herbs. Cook for 5 minutes more. Serve immediately.

Tip If making this soup using canned beans, be sure to rinse and drain them well to remove excess sodium before adding to the pan.

NUTRITION STATS *per 1/10 recipe*

Calories 260; **Fat** 4.5 g; **Sodium** 240 mg; **Carbs** 31 g; **Fibre** 7 g; **Protein** 25 g

Jamie with her mom, Patti.

Jamie Salé

Born: Calgary, AB

Played: Olympic gold medallist (2002) and first-place World Figure Skating champion (2001)

Fact: Soup making is a family affair in the Salé family, and on cold Alberta days they gather in the kitchen to make Grammie's (Jamie's mom's) chicken soup. It's warming and full of goodness.

Pho Bucket Soup

Pho is traditionally served in a very large soup bowl. We've seen some the size of a hockey helmet, thus the "bucket" take on our version! Depending on the size of the person and the size of the "bucket," you may want to adjust the amount of broth.

Serves: 1
Prep: 5 min.
Cook: 2 min.

2 cups (500 mL)	no-salt-added chicken or beef broth
1 tbsp (15 mL)	freshly squeezed lemon juice
½ tsp (2.5 mL)	reduced-sodium soy sauce (look for gluten-free)
½ cup (125 mL)	cooked rice noodles or gluten-free spaghetti
½ cup (125 mL)	cooked chicken or beef, thinly sliced
¼ cup (60 mL)	bean sprouts and/or grated carrots
1 tbsp (15 mL)	chopped green onions
1 tsp (5 mL)	minced fresh basil leaves (optional)
1 tsp (5 mL)	minced fresh mint leaves (optional)
1 tsp (5 mL)	minced fresh cilantro leaves (optional)

1. In a saucepan over medium-high heat, bring broth to a boil. Reduce heat, stir in lemon juice and soy sauce, and simmer for 2 minutes.

2. Meanwhile, place noodles in a large soup bowl. Layer meat, bean sprouts, and carrots, and top with green onions. Pour over hot broth. Sprinkle with herbs (if using).

MAKE-AHEAD

Up to 2 days in advance, store pre-assembled noodle bowls in the fridge—just add hot broth for ready-to-go pho.

VARIATION

Instead of using hot broth, toss noodle mixture with 2 tbsp (30 mL) Visor-Foggin' Asian Dressing (page 155) for a cold salad.

Tip Keep bean sprouts crisp and fresh by storing them in a bowl of water in the fridge. Just be sure to change the water daily.

NUTRITION STATS per 1 recipe
(using no-salt-added chicken broth)

Calories 260; **Fat** 5 g; **Sodium** 270 mg; **Carbs** 27 g; **Fibre** 2 g; **Protein** 23 g

Frozen Peas

Green peas are small but packed with plenty of health benefits. This most nutritious legume has a relatively high protein level and is a great source of bone-building vitamin K and manganese. It is also high in folate—which helps support a healthy heart—and has over 4 g of fibre per ½ cup (125 mL).

Peas are an essential freezer item not only for cooking but also for injury relief. A bag of frozen peas moulds to even the most difficult-to-reach areas. We keep an injury bag of peas labelled and well away from the one that is for consumption.

Frozen peas can be added straight from the freezer to cool down and add bright colour to hot soups like Grammie Salé's Chicken Soup (page 186) or Tessa Virtue's World Champion Chili (page 228), Quinoa Bowls (pages 232–239), and slow cooker stews like Beauty Butter Chicken (page 202). Green peas also add fibre, protein, and vitamins to Sniper Smoothies (pages 60–81)!

Adding 1 cup (250 mL) puréed peas to guacamole not only boosts protein, flavour, and texture but also stretches the quantity of an otherwise fairly pricey avocado.

Designing soup can be a sport unto itself! Puréed or chunky? Chicken or beef? Quinoa or noodles? Broccoli or kale? The combinations are endless and the benefits are incredible: warming the body after cold days on the ice … nourishing and replenishing lost nutrients with fluids and vegetables. What will your player choose?

Combine one ingredient from each row below in a saucepan and heat through.

Liquid (2 cups/500 mL)	Beef broth (reduced-sodium)	Chicken broth (reduced-sodium)	Vegetable broth (reduced-sodium)	Tomato juice (reduced-sodium)	¼ cup (60 mL) lite coconut milk diluted with water to equal 2 cups (500 mL)
Veggies (1 cup/250 mL)	Tomatoes, diced	Sweet peppers, carrots, or celery, chopped	Broccoli florets, fresh or frozen	Baby spinach leaves	Peas or corn, frozen
Carb (¼ cup/60 mL)	Quinoa, cooked	Pasta, cooked	Black beans (rinsed and drained if canned)	Rice noodles, cooked	Barley, cooked
Protein (2 oz/60 g)	Beef, cooked	Shrimp, cooked	Quinoa, cooked	Tofu (firm)	Chicken, cooked
Seasoning (to taste)	Fresh herbs (basil, parsley, cilantro), chopped				

Dinner Dangles

We asked the moms, dads, and wives of the pros to share their favourite and most-requested recipes. They responded with a wide range of dishes. We made them all and they are truly delicious.

Erik with his wife, Ryan.

Erik Condra

Born: Trenton, Michigan

Played: Ottawa

Fact: Erik loves to eat this flavourful orzo dish the night before a big game, usually accompanied by a piece of chicken or fish. It's a filling meal that doesn't sit heavy in his stomach, and it gives him the energy he needs to hit the ice.

Condra's Shot-Blocking Orzo

Condra is no stranger to positioning himself in front of flying pucks (shot-blocking) to help out the defence. This dish is delicious hot, but equally good served cold the next day (if you have any leftovers!). It's the most requested side dish in the Condra home, especially after Erik returns from a long road trip.

Serves: 6
Prep: 5 min.
Cook: 15 min.
Stand: 2 min.

2½ cups (625 mL)	water
1 cup (250 mL)	dried orzo pasta
2 tbsp (30 mL)	olive oil
1 tsp (5 mL)	dried mint
1 tsp (5 mL)	sea salt
½ tsp (2.5 mL)	paprika
pinch	finely grated lemon zest
3	chopped green onions
	Juice of ½ lemon

1. In a saucepan over medium-high heat, combine water, orzo, oil, mint, salt, paprika, and lemon zest and bring to a boil. Reduce heat and simmer for 12 to 15 minutes or until orzo is tender, stirring frequently. (Orzo will have a soupy look, more like a risotto.)

2. Remove from heat. Let stand for 2 minutes, and then gently stir in green onions and lemon juice. Serve immediately.

Tip *If you can, use 1 tbsp (15 mL) fresh mint instead of dried. Stir in with green onions and lemon juice in step 2.*

NUTRITION STATS *per ⅙ recipe*
Calories 160; **Fat** 5 g; **Sodium** 420 mg; **Carbs** 23 g; **Fibre** 1 g; **Protein** 4 g

Yorky's Checking Chicken Tacos

Serves: 6
Prep: 5 min.
Cook: 4 hr.
Note: This recipe requires a slow cooker.

Jason York is known as a reliable checking defenceman (eliminating opposing players to score). You will find this chicken recipe to be amazingly reliable, easy, and delicious. Five minutes in the morning with the slow cooker, and dinner will be ready when you are.

6	boneless, skinless chicken breasts
1 package (1.25 oz/35 g)	reduced-sodium taco seasoning
1 jar (15.5 oz/439.4 g)	salsa (mild, medium, or hot)
	Large flour tortillas

Toppings

Shredded lettuce, diced avocados or Redden's Rippin' Guacamole (page 128), Heatley's Light the Lamp Salsa (page 131) or diced tomatoes, minced green onions, shredded cheese

1. In a slow cooker, place all of the ingredients in the order listed.

2. Cook on Low for 4 hours. When ready, chicken shreds easily. Remove lid and, using two forks, shred chicken to desired consistency. Keep on Warm until serving time. Serve with your favourite toppings.

Tip Use Yorky's taco chicken as a topping for Mexican Quinoa Bowl (page 244).

NUTRITION STATS *per 100 g*
Calories 90; **Fat** 1.5 g; **Sodium** 560 mg; **Carbs** 4 g; **Fibre** 2 g; **Protein** 14 g

Jason with his wife, Laurel.

Jason York

Born: Nepean, ON

Played: Detroit, Anaheim, Ottawa, Nashville, Boston

Fact: The Yorks love these tacos—they are fun to assemble and make a great sit-down family meal.

Bobby Ryan's Comin'-in-Hot Sweet-&-Sour Chicken

Serves: 4 to 6
Prep: 15 min.
Cook: 1 hr. 8 min.

Known for his incredible agility and ability to score goals, it is no wonder Bobby Ryan's tagline is "comin'-in-hot"! Bobby loves to indulge in this homemade version of Chinese sweet-&-sour chicken. Danielle Rhodes says this is first on the list of meals Bobby requests when they get back home from being away.

4	boneless, skinless chicken breasts, cut into 1-inch (2.5 cm) cubes
	Salt and pepper
1 cup (250 mL)	cornstarch
2	large eggs
¼ cup (60 mL)	vegetable oil
¾ cup (175 mL)	granulated sugar
¼ cup (60 mL)	low-sodium ketchup
½ cup (125 mL)	white vinegar
1 tbsp (15 mL)	reduced-sodium soy sauce (look for gluten-free)
1 tsp (5 mL)	garlic powder

1. Preheat oven to 325°F (160°C). Grease a 13- by 9-inch (33 by 23 cm) glass baking dish.

2. Season chicken with salt and pepper to taste.

3. Prepare breading station: In a shallow dish, place cornstarch. In another shallow dish, beat eggs.

4. Dip chicken in cornstarch and then eggs. Set aside.

5. In a large saucepan over medium-high heat, heat oil. In batches, cook chicken about 2 minutes per side or until browned but not cooked through. Transfer browned chicken to prepared baking dish.

6. In a medium bowl, whisk together sugar, ketchup, vinegar, soy sauce, and garlic powder. Pour evenly over chicken. Bake for 1 hour or until sauce is reduced and sticks to chicken, turning chicken every 15 minutes.

7. Serve over brown or white rice.

Bobby and his wife, Danielle.

Bobby Ryan

Born: Cherry Hill, New Jersey

Played: Anaheim, Ottawa

Fact: Bobby's fiancé, Danielle, makes this for Bobby when he's craving a "cheat" meal—it's packed with flavour without being processed.

NUTRITION STATS   *per ⅙ recipe*

Calories 460;   **Fat** 14 g;   **Sodium** 680 mg;   **Carbs** 48 g;   **Fibre** 0 g;   **Protein** 33 g

Beauty Butter Chicken

Serves: 6 to 8
Prep: 10 min.
Cook: 4 to 10 hr.
Note: This recipe requires a slow cooker.

The ingredient list may look long, but it doesn't take much time to put everything together—and then you can walk away while the slow cooker does the rest. It's a beauty of a recipe and delicious served with jasmine or basmati rice.

5 cloves	garlic, minced
1 can (28 oz/796 mL)	reduced-sodium diced tomatoes, with juice
1 can (5.5 oz/156 mL)	tomato paste
2 tbsp (30 mL)	butter, melted
2 tsp (10 mL)	ground ginger
2 tsp (10 mL)	curry powder
1 tsp (5 mL)	ground cumin
1 tsp (5 mL)	ground cinnamon
1 tsp (5 mL)	ground coriander
¼ tsp (1 mL)	ground cardamom
1 lb (500 g)	skinless chicken thighs (with or without bone, about 6 to 8 pieces)
2 cups (500 mL)	grated carrots
1 tbsp (15 mL)	freshly squeezed lime juice
1 cup (250 mL)	3% plain Greek yogurt or sour cream
	Chopped toasted unsalted cashews
	Chopped fresh cilantro leaves

1. In a slow cooker, combine garlic, tomatoes, tomato paste, butter, spices, chicken, and carrots. Stir well.

2. Cook on High for 4 to 6 hours or on Low for 8 to 10 hours. When ready, chicken shreds easily.

3. Stir in lime juice and yogurt. Garnish with cashews and cilantro.

MAKE-AHEAD

Make up little packages of this spice mixture in advance, for when you need a last-minute dinner idea.

NUTRITION STATS *per ⅛ recipe*

Calories 380; **Fat** 18 g; **Sodium** 270 mg; **Carbs** 19 g; **Fibre** 4 g; **Protein** 38 g

Daniel with his mom, Margareta, and sister, Cecilia.

Daniel Alfredsson

Born: Gothenburg, Sweden

Played: Ottawa, Detroit

Fact: Daniel's wife, Bibbi, fuels all four of their growing boys and Daniel with authentic Swedish comfort food.

Alfie's Power-Play Meat Sauce

Having the man advantage on the ice (power play) opens up scoring chances. This authentic Swedish meat sauce will score big—it's especially good served over gluten-free noodles. You may find that there are extra players around when they hear what's for dinner.

Serves: *6 to 8*
Prep: *10 min.*
Cook: *45 to 55 min.*

1 tbsp (15 mL)	butter
1 lb (500 g)	lean ground beef
1 tbsp (15 mL)	olive oil
3 strips (3.5 oz/100 g)	bacon, chopped
1 cup (250 mL)	mushrooms, chopped
4 cloves	garlic, minced
1	large carrot, finely chopped
2 tsp (10 mL)	tomato paste
1 lb (500 g)	reduced-sodium crushed tomatoes, with juice
	Salt and pepper

1. In a Dutch oven or heavy-bottomed saucepan over high heat, melt butter. Add beef and cook until browned. Transfer beef (including pan drippings) to a bowl and set aside.

2. In the same pot, heat oil. Cook bacon, mushrooms, garlic, and carrots for 5 minutes or until lightly softened. Stir in tomato paste.

3. Return beef and drippings to pot. Stir in tomatoes and season with salt and pepper to taste. Reduce heat and simmer for 30 to 40 minutes or until carrots are fork-tender and sauce has thickened.

NUTRITION STATS *per 7 oz (200 g)*
Calories 340; **Fat** 14 g; **Sodium** 540 mg; **Carbs** 28 g; **Fibre** 3 g; **Protein** 24 g

Serves: 6
Prep: 15 min.
Cook: 40 min.

Alfie's Swedish Meatballs

Everyone loves Swedish meatballs, especially when the recipe comes from Sweden! Bibbi loves to make this recipe for Daniel, served with mashed potatoes, lingonberries, and a big green salad.

¼ cup (60 mL)	dried bread crumbs (look for gluten-free)
6 tbsp (90 mL)	water
1	small onion, finely chopped
2 lb (1 kg)	lean ground beef
½ cup (125 mL)	10% cream
2	large eggs
	Salt and pepper
2 tbsp (30 mL)	butter
Additional 2 cups (500 mL)	water

1. In a large bowl, soak bread crumbs in water for 2 minutes. Add onion, ground beef, cream, and eggs, and season with salt and pepper to taste. Stir until smooth. Using your hands, form small meatballs (about 1 inch/2.5 cm in diameter) and set aside.

2. In a Dutch oven or heavy-bottomed saucepan over low heat, melt 1 tbsp (15 mL) butter. Remove from heat and reserve.

3. In a frying pan over medium heat, melt remaining butter. Working in batches so as not to overcrowd the pan, brown meatballs. Transfer browned meatballs to reserved pan. Add 2 cups (500 mL) water to the frying pan and, using a wooden spoon, stir up all the browned bits from the bottom of the pan. Pour over meatballs.

4. Cover and cook meatballs, over medium-high heat, for 30 minutes or until internal temperature reaches 165°F (74°C). Transfer meatballs to a plate, and use the liquid to make a gravy. Return meatballs to the sauce to keep warm until serving time.

Tip To make gravy, stir ¼ cup (60 mL) all-purpose flour into ¼ cup (60 mL) cold broth or water until smooth. Whisk into hot liquid, stirring constantly, over medium-high heat until mixture begins to thicken, about 8 minutes.

NUTRITION STATS *per 100 g*
(using 10% cream and lean ground beef)

Calories 150; **Fat** 9 g; **Sodium** 160 mg; **Carbs** 3 g; **Fibre** 0 g; **Protein** 14 g

Daniel's parents, Hasse and Margareta.

Daniel Alfredsson

Born: Gothenburg, Sweden

Played: Ottawa, Detroit

Fact: The Alfredsson familiy loves to prepare authentic Swedish meatballs. It's hard to keep the four boys' hands out of the pot!

Fisher's Slap-Shot Spaghetti Casserole

Serves: 6 to 8
Prep: 15 min.
Cook: 45 to 50 min.
Stand: 15 min.

It is an exciting moment to watch Mike Fisher unleash a slap shot, and seeing his mom's famous spaghetti casserole on the dinner table ranks right up there, too! This twist on family-favourite spaghetti and meat sauce is a winner.

1 tbsp (15 mL)	butter
2 cups (500 mL)	sliced mushrooms
1 cup (250 mL)	chopped onion
1 cup (250 mL)	chopped green pepper
1 can (28 oz/796 mL)	whole tomatoes, with juice
1 package (5 g)	beef bouillon powder
½ cup (125 mL)	sliced black olives, drained
2 tsp (10 mL)	dried oregano
½ tsp (2.5 mL)	sea salt
¼ tsp (1 mL)	freshly ground black pepper
1 lb (500 g)	ground beef, browned and drained (optional)
12 oz (375 g)	spaghetti, cooked and drained
2 cups (500 mL)	shredded cheddar cheese, divided
1 can (10 oz/284 mL)	cream of mushroom soup
¼ cup (60 mL)	water
¼ cup (60 mL)	freshly grated Parmesan cheese

Mike with his mom, Karen.

Mike Fisher

Born: Peterborough, ON

Played: Ottawa, Nashville

Fact: Like every other hockey player, Mike eats a lot of pasta. His mom, Karen, came up with this creative twist on a classic to feed her houseful of athletes.

1. In a large deep frying pan over high heat, melt butter. Sauté mushrooms, onion, and green pepper for 5 minutes or until tender. Stir in tomatoes, bouillon, olives, oregano, salt, and pepper. Stir in ground beef (if using). Reduce heat and simmer for 10 minutes.

2. Preheat oven to 350°F (180°C). Grease a 13- by 9-inch (33 by 23 cm) glass baking dish.

3. Place half of the spaghetti in baking dish. Top with half of the sauce. Sprinkle with 1 cup (250 mL) cheddar cheese. Repeat layers.

4. In a bowl, combine soup and water until smooth. Pour over top of casserole. Sprinkle with Parmesan. Bake, uncovered, for 30 to 35 minutes or until heated through and cheese is melted. Remove from oven and let stand for 15 minutes before serving.

VARIATION

Substitute 2 cups (500 mL) diced cooked chicken for the ground beef. Stir into fully cooked sauce just before assembling casserole.

Tip *Letting the casserole cool before serving will help cut pieces keep their shape.*

NUTRITION STATS *per 1 cup (250 mL)*

Calories 280; **Fat** 14 g; **Sodium** 810 mg; **Carbs** 19 g; **Fibre** 2 g; **Protein** 20 g

Captain Yzerman Lasagna

Serves: 6 to 8
Prep: 30 min.
Bake: 30 min.
Stand: 10 min.

Never underestimate the power of home-cooked and reliable meals like lasagna! Players miss special simple meals when on the road. There are many reasons to visit home, and mom's lasagna makes it feel like you never left—just ask The Captain (Steve Yzerman)!

1 package (9 oz/255 g)	lasagna noodles, cooked

Meat sauce

1½ lb (750 g)	lean ground beef
1 clove	garlic, minced
1 tbsp (15 mL)	dried basil
1 tsp (5 mL)	sea salt
2 cans (5.5 fl oz/156 mL)	tomato paste
½ cup (125 mL)	water
1⅓ cups (325 mL)	crushed tomatoes, with juices

Cheese filling

3 cups (750 mL)	creamed cottage cheese
½ cup (125 mL)	freshly grated Parmesan cheese
2	large eggs
2 tbsp (30 mL)	dried parsley flakes
½ tsp (2.5 mL)	freshly ground black pepper
7 oz (210 g)	sliced mozzarella cheese

1. **Make meat sauce:** In a large frying pan or saucepan, over medium-high heat, brown beef. Spoon off fat. Add garlic, basil, salt, tomato paste, water, and crushed tomatoes. Stir to combine. Bring to a boil, then reduce heat and simmer, uncovered, for 30 minutes or until some of the liquid has evaporated, stirring occasionally.

2. **Make cheese filling:** Meanwhile, in a medium bowl, combine cottage cheese, Parmesan, eggs, parsley, and pepper.

3. Preheat oven to 375°F (190°C). Lightly grease a 13- by 9-inch (33 by 23 cm) glass baking dish or lasagna pan.

Steve Yzerman

Born: Cranbrook, B.C.

Played: Detroit, Tampa

Fact: Steve's mom, Jean, says this is Steve's favourite recipe—he asks for it whenever he comes home to visit.

4. Assemble: Place one-third of the lasagna noodles (about 5) in the bottom of the baking dish, overlapping edges of noodles. Cover with one-third of the meat sauce, then one-third of the cheese filling, and then one-third of the mozzarella cheese. Repeat twice. Bake for 30 minutes or until cheese is melted and lasagna is heated through. Let stand 10 minutes before cutting.

NUTRITION STATS   *per 250 g*

Calories 410;   **Fat** 17 g;   **Sodium** 890 mg;   **Carbs** 25 g;   **Fibre** 3 g;   **Protein** 39 g

Turris's Top-Shelf Alfredo

Serves: *4 to 6*
Prep: *15 min.*
Cook: *35 to 40 min.*

Into the net above the goalie's shoulder (top shelf) is Kyle Turris's sweet spot for goal-scoring. We think endless practice and oodles of noodles, chicken, and cream help him hit the mark.

1 package (16 oz/454 g)	dried bow-tie pasta
1 tbsp (15 mL)	butter
1	shallot, finely chopped
1 clove	garlic, finely chopped
	Salt and pepper
1 tsp (5 mL)	ground nutmeg
2 cups (500 mL)	35% whipping cream, divided
2 cups (500 mL)	freshly grated Parmesan cheese, divided
4 to 6	boneless, skinless chicken breasts (about 6 oz/175 g each)
1 tbsp (15 mL)	coconut oil

Kyle with his wife, Julie.

Kyle Turris

Born: New Westminster, B.C.

Played: Ottawa, Phoenix

Fact: Kyle often eats Alfredo with chicken 8 hours before game time for his pre-game meal to keep his weight up. Because of his fast metabolism and all the calories he burns on the ice, he needs a good balance of protein and carbs for energy.

1. In a large pot of boiling salted water, cook pasta according to package directions.

2. Meanwhile, in a large saucepan over medium heat, melt butter. Add shallots, garlic, salt and pepper to taste, and nutmeg. Cook for 3 minutes or until shallots are translucent. Reduce heat to medium-low. Add ½ cup (125 mL) cream and bring to a boil. When cream foams, add ½ cup (125 mL) more cream and bring to a boil. When cream again foams, add remaining 1 cup (250 mL) cream and ½ cup (125 mL) Parmesan. Reduce heat to low.

3. Drain pasta, reserving about 1 tbsp (15 mL) of pasta water. Return noodles and reserved water to the pot. Add cream mixture and remaining Parmesan. Stir to combine, cover, and set aside.

4. Season chicken with salt and pepper to taste. In a medium saucepan over medium heat, melt coconut oil. Add chicken and cook for 4 minutes on each side or until browned and cooked to an internal temperature of 165°F (74°C).

5. To serve, divide prepared pasta among serving plates. Top each with a cooked chicken breast and sprinkle with extra Parmesan.

NUTRITION STATS   *per ⅙ recipe*

Calories 620;   **Fat** 40 g;   **Sodium** 640 mg;   **Carbs** 33 g;   **Fibre** 2 g;   **Protein** 30 g

Sweet Potatoes

Sweet potatoes contain about twice as much fibre as other potatoes, aiding in satiety and hunger levels. They are also rich in potassium, vitamin B6, manganese (controls blood sugar levels), vitamins C and E (antioxidants needed for disease prevention), magnesium (aids in relaxation), vitamin D (encourages healthy bones, nerves, skin, and teeth), and iron—all essential for the active and developing player.

Sweet potatoes should be a must-have in every hockey family's meal plan. Not only are they available year-round, but they are inexpensive and versatile, too. Try them cubed and roasted, cut into wedges and baked, cut into

medallions and grilled, or (peeled or unpeeled) cooked and mashed (like P.K. Subban, page 44). Add them to Quick-Hands Hummus (page 123), Neil-er's Takedown Vegetable Soup (page 178), Zamboni Soup (page 185), and slow cooker stews like Beauty Butter Chicken (page 200). Puréed sweet potatoes can even be added to baked goods, mac 'n' cheese, and Sniper Smoothies (pages 60–81).

Here are some of our favourite quick and easy ways to prepare sweet potatoes, either to enjoy on their own or to add to your player's pre-game meal of choice.

Baked: Preheat oven to 400°F (200°C). Scrub potatoes well, and pierce each several times with the tines of a fork. Place on a rimmed baking sheet lined with foil. Bake until tender, about 45 minutes. Alternately, microwave on High for 4 to 5 minutes, turn, and microwave an additional 4 to 5 minutes, or until tender. Slice each sweet potato lengthwise and top with butter, Heatley's Light the Lamp Salsa (page 131), or a topping of your choice. You can also let cool slightly and mash for use in recipes, or enjoy with butter, salt, and pepper.

Roasted Cubes: Preheat oven to 450°F (230°C). In a large mixing bowl, combine 2 cups (500 mL) cubed sweet potatoes, 1 tbsp (15 mL) olive oil, 1 clove garlic (minced), and toss. Arrange potato mixture in a single layer on a heavyweight rimmed baking sheet or in a 13- by 9- by 2-inch (33 by 23 by 5 cm) baking dish. Place on top rack of oven and bake about 35 minutes, or until tender and slightly browned.

Baked Sweet Potato Sticks: Preheat oven to 450°F (230°C). Peel and slice large sweet potato into long thin strips, about ½ inch by 3 inches (1.25 by 7.5 cm). Toss with 1 tbsp (15 mL) olive oil. Place sweet potatoes on a rimmed baking sheet lined with foil. Bake for a total of 25 to 30 minutes. After the first 15 minutes, remove baking sheet from oven and turn the potatoes. Return to oven and bake for another 10 to 15 minutes, or until they are browned. Let cool for 5 minutes before serving.

Phillips's Stay-at-Home Penne

Serves: *4 to 6*
Prep: *5 min.*
Cook: *20 to 25 min.*

Chris "stays at home" to defend his goalie and shut down the opponent. His go-to meal may seem an unlikely pre-game choice, but the alcohol burns off during cooking, leaving only a delicious flavour.

1 package (16 oz/454 g)	dried penne pasta
2 tbsp (30 mL)	butter
¼ lb (125 g)	thinly sliced pancetta, chopped
⅓ cup (75 mL)	vodka
1½ cups (375 mL)	reduced-sodium tomato sauce
½ cup (125 mL)	35% whipping cream
½ cup (125 mL)	freshly grated Parmesan cheese

1. In a large pot of boiling salted water, cook pasta according to package directions. Drain and set aside.

2. Meanwhile, in a large frying pan over medium heat, melt butter. Add pancetta and sauté for 2 minutes or until lightly browned. Increase heat to high, add vodka, and, stirring constantly, cook for 4 to 5 minutes or until reduced by half. Stir in tomato sauce and then whipping cream. Reduce heat to low and simmer, uncovered, for 10 to 12 minutes or until some of the liquid has evaporated, stirring occasionally.

3. Add pasta. Toss together and heat through. Serve topped with Parmesan.

NUTRITION STATS *per ⅙ recipe*

Calories 380; **Fat** 19 g; **Sodium** 900 mg; **Carbs** 33 g; **Fibre** 3 g; **Protein** 12 g

Chris with his mom, Carol.

Chris Phillips

Born: Calgary, AB

Played: Ottawa

Fact: Chris's mom always made him pasta the night before a game, and now Erin continues the tradition. Chris loves to pair his pasta with a great steak.

On-the-Fly Ragout

Just like coaches make player substitutions while the game is underway, this recipe lends itself to switching up ingredients in the moment—depending on your situation and what's in the fridge or pantry. See what winning combinations inspire you on the fly.

Serves: 6, with leftovers
Prep: 10 min.
Cook: 25 min.

1 lb (500 g)	honey garlic or mild Italian sausages, casings removed
2 cloves	garlic, minced
1	large onion, thinly sliced crosswise
2 stalks	celery, thinly sliced
1 or 2	large red or yellow peppers, thinly sliced
1 can (28 oz/796 mL)	reduced-sodium diced tomatoes, with juice

1. In a large saucepan over medium-high heat, sauté sausage, garlic, onion, and celery for 8 minutes or until sausage is browned and onion is soft (use the back of a wooden spoon to break up the sausage as it cooks). Add peppers and sauté for 2 minutes. Stir in tomatoes. Bring to a boil, reduce heat to low, and simmer for 15 minutes or until flavours come together.

2. Serve over quinoa or brown rice.

NUTRITION STATS   *per ⅙ recipe*

Calories 210;   **Fat** 11 g;   **Sodium** 220 mg;   **Carbs** 12 g;   **Fibre** 3 g;   **Protein** 14 g

Captain Campbell's Slow Cooker Cacciatore

Serves: 6
Prep: 15 min.
Cook: 5 to 8 hr.
Note: This recipe requires a slow cooker.

Italian food—Canadian team captain style. This delicious one-dish chicken and veggie dinner needs only a side of pasta and *buon appetito*! Cassie Campbell knows a winning combination when she sees one.

2 cups (500 mL)	sliced fresh mushrooms
3	large carrots, coarsely chopped
½ cup (125 mL)	julienned red pepper
½ cup (125 mL)	julienned green pepper
1	small onion, chopped
1 clove	garlic, minced
¼ cup (60 mL)	Italian salad dressing
5 or 6	boneless, skinless chicken breasts, halved
1 tsp (5 mL)	dried thyme leaves
1 can (19 fl oz/540 mL)	reduced-sodium crushed or diced tomatoes, with juice

1. In a slow cooker, combine mushrooms, carrots, peppers, onion, and garlic.

2. In a large frying pan over medium-high heat, heat dressing. Working in batches, cook chicken for 3 to 4 minutes per side or until browned. Place on top of vegetables in slow cooker. Drizzle with drippings from pan.

3. Combine thyme with tomatoes. Pour over chicken. Cover slow cooker and cook on High for 5 hours or on Low for 6 to 8 hours or until chicken is cooked to an internal temperate of 165°F (74°C) and the vegetables are fork-tender. Note: If sauce isn't thick enough, remove lid and cook on High for an additional 15 to 20 minutes so that the liquid evaporates. Additionally, sauce can be thickened by stirring together 2 tbsp (30 mL) cornstarch and ¼ cup (60 mL) cold water and then adding mixture to sauce in slow cooker. Cook on High with lid off for 15 minutes more.

4. Serve on baby spinach, if desired, with pasta, brown rice, or quinoa.

NUTRITION STATS *per ⅙ recipe*

Calories 220; **Fat** 7 g; **Sodium** 170 mg; **Carbs** 14 g; **Fibre** 3 g; **Protein** 25 g

Cassie Campbell

Born: Richmond Hill, ON

Played: Team Canada 1998, 2002, 2006

Fact: Cassie loves to cook for her family and knows that even with her crazy schedule, nutrition and flavour must be a priority.

Korey's Chicken Parmesan

Once you're into the egg-dipping and breading, go big! Make extra batches of this recipe, and freeze the cooked chicken breasts individually for last-minute meals. Serve with gluten-free noodles and green salad.

Serves: 4
Prep: 10 min.
Cook: 20 to 25 min.

4	boneless, skinless chicken breasts, flattened
3 or 4	large eggs
2 cups (500 mL)	dried bread crumbs (look for gluten-free)
¼ cup (60 mL)	ground flaxseeds
¼ cup (60 mL)	freshly grated Parmesan cheese
2 cups (500 mL)	reduced-sodium tomato sauce
	Shredded cheese (Parmesan, mozzarella, or your favourite)

1. Preheat oven to 375°F (190°C). Line a baking pan with aluminum foil.

2. Prepare breading station: In a shallow dish, beat eggs well. In another shallow dish, combine bread crumbs, flaxseeds, and Parmesan.

3. Dip chicken in egg and coat well, allowing excess to drip off. Press both sides of chicken into crumb mixture. Place on prepared baking pan. Bake for 20 minutes or until chicken reaches an internal temperature of 165°F (74°C).

4. Remove from oven. Top with tomato sauce and cheese, and return to oven to bake for 5 minutes more or until cheese is melted.

Tip To flatten chicken breasts, place them between two sheets of waxed or parchment paper. Using the flat side of a mallet, a heavy rolling pin, or even a large can, lightly pound or press to about ¼ inch (0.6 cm) thickness.

NUTRITION STATS *per ¼ recipe*

Calories 440; **Fat** 14 g; **Sodium** 960 mg; **Carbs** 35 g; **Fibre** 4 g; **Protein** 42 g

Giroux's Give-'n'-Go Chicken

Serves: 4
Prep: 15 min.
Cook: 16 to 20 min.

Claude Giroux dresses it up on the ice and at mealtime. This delicious chicken gives him the get-up-and-go to "give 'n' go" (pass the puck and receive it back).

6 oz (175 g)	creamy goat cheese
2 cloves	garlic, minced
1	green onion, finely chopped
1 tsp (5 mL)	dried thyme
½ tsp (2.5 mL)	dried marjoram
1 pinch	cayenne pepper
4	boneless, skinless chicken breasts
2 tbsp (30 mL)	olive oil
½ tsp (2.5 mL)	paprika
½ tsp (2.5 mL)	ground cumin
¼ tsp (1 mL)	sea salt
¼ tsp (1 mL)	freshly ground black pepper

1. In a small bowl, combine goat cheese, garlic, green onion, thyme, marjoram, and cayenne pepper until smooth. Set aside.

2. Starting from thinnest side, cut each chicken breast in half horizontally and open flat. Spread one-quarter of cheese mixture on one half of each breast, cover with other half of breast, and secure with toothpicks. Repeat with remaining chicken.

3. Preheat barbecue to medium-high.

4. In a small bowl, combine oil, paprika, cumin, salt, and pepper. Brush over chicken breasts.

5. Grease grill.

6. Grill chicken (close lid) for 8 minutes. Turn chicken over and grill for 8 minutes more or until meat is no longer pink in the middle and internal temperature reaches 165°F (74°C). Serve with quinoa or pasta and spinach or with PASS Salad (page 139).

Claude with his mom, Nicole.

Claude Giroux

Born: Hearst, ON

Played: Philadelphia

Fact: Claude likes to eat this chicken dish after his workouts because it delivers lots of protein and tastes great!

NUTRITION STATS *per ¼ recipe*

Calories 510; **Fat** 23 g; **Sodium** 470 mg; **Carbs** 1 g; **Fibre** 0 g; **Protein** 69 g

Erin's Coach's Mexican Casserole

Serves: 8
Prep: 15 min.
Cook: 1 hr.
Stand: 10 min.

This free-form enchilada was a family favourite when Erin was growing up. She's now adopted her mom's recipe and makes it a lot when Chris's teammates come over. It's very filling—and those boys can eat! Erin serves this with Clutch Caesar Salad (page 140).

1½ lb (750 g)	lean ground beef
1 cup (250 mL)	diced onion
1 clove	garlic, minced
1½ cups (375 mL)	finely chopped red pepper
1½ cups (375 mL)	hot salsa
1 package (10 oz/238 g)	frozen spinach
1 can (8 oz/227 g)	reduced-sodium tomato sauce
10	large flour tortillas (10 inches/25 cm)
2 cups (500 mL)	sour cream, divided
2 cups (500 mL)	shredded cheese (Monterey and cheddar)
3 cups (750 mL)	shredded lettuce
2 cups (500 mL)	diced fresh tomatoes
2 cups (500 mL)	diced avocado
¼ cup (60 mL)	sliced Kalamata olives (optional)

1. In a large saucepan over medium-high heat, brown beef, onions, and garlic for 8 minutes or until beef is no longer pink. Drain liquid, and return pan to heat.

2. Stir in red peppers and cook for 5 minutes. Stir in salsa, spinach, and tomato sauce, and bring to a light boil. Reduce heat and simmer for 20 minutes or until liquid has evaporated (meat sauce should be thick).

3. Preheat oven to 350°F (180°C).

4. Line an 8-cup (2 L) casserole dish with 6 flour tortillas, ensuring that tortillas cover bottom and hang over side of dish (these brown and are yummy for dipping). Spoon half the chili meat sauce into dish and top with 1 cup (250 mL) sour cream. Layer remaining 4 tortillas over filling and overlapping the lower shells. Spoon on remaining chili meat sauce and remaining 1 cup (250 mL) sour cream.

5. Bake for 25 to 30 minutes or until heated through. Let stand 10 minutes. Top with cheese, lettuce, tomatoes, avocado, and olives (if using). Slice and serve.

NUTRITION STATS   *per ¹/₁₀ recipe*

Calories 470;   **Fat** 20 g;   **Sodium** 1580 mg;   **Carbs** 49 g;   **Fibre** 8 g;   **Protein** 24 g

Tessa Virtue's World Champion Chili

Serves: 6
Prep: 10 min.
Cook: 30 min.

How do you fuel a world champion figure skater? With a huge pot of chili, of course! This tasty basic recipe starts you off right. Enjoy it as is, or rev it up with additions of grated carrots, corn, or any other of your favourite veggies. Serve with shredded cheese, green onions, and hot sauce.

1 lb (500 mL)	extra lean ground beef or turkey
1	onion, diced
2	red or yellow peppers, diced
1 package (1.25 oz/35 g)	reduced-sodium chili seasoning
1 can (28 oz/796 mL)	reduced-sodium diced tomatoes, with juice
1 can (19 oz/540 mL)	red or white kidney beans, rinsed and drained

1. In a Dutch oven or heavy-bottomed saucepan, over high heat, cook beef for 5 minutes or until browned. Add onion and peppers and cook for 5 minutes or until slightly softened. Stir in chili seasoning to coat mixture. Add tomatoes and beans. Bring to a boil, then reduce heat to medium-low and simmer for 20 minutes or until liquid is reduced and chili is thickened.

2. Serve immediately.

Tip Add a layer of chili to burritos, dips, or Erin's Coach's Mexican Casserole (page 224), or a ladleful to quinoa, rice, or soup.

NUTRITION STATS   *per 250 mL*

Calories 240;   **Fat** 8 g;   **Sodium** 160 mg;   **Carbs** 24 g;   **Fibre** 6 g;   **Protein** 20 g

Myra Klarman

Tessa Virtue

Born: London, ON

Played: Olympic figure
skater (gold medal 2010;
silver medal 2014)

Fact: Tessa thinks there's
nothing better or more
comforting than finishing
a long day of training in a
cold rink with a warm bowl
of chili. Bonus: It's easy to
make and there are always
leftovers!

A young Nick with his mom, Janis.

Nick Foligno

Born: Buffalo, NY

Played: Ottawa, Columbus

Fact: This recipe was passed on to Nick's wife, Janelle, by Nick's mom, Janis. It has fuelled a family of hockey stars: Nick's brother Marcus currently plays in Buffalo, and his father, Mike, played in the league for 15 years (for Detroit Buffalo, Toronto, and Florida). Nick shares this recipe in loving memory of his wonderful mother.

Foligno's Just-in-Game-Time Pasta Sauce

Start with three ingredients and a slow cooker in the morning, and by late afternoon, you've got a fantastic, different-from-your-average meat sauce. Serve it over macaroni and this hearty game-day meal will be a sure hit with the hockey player in your house, says Janelle Foligno.

Serves: 8
Prep: 15 min.
Cook: 4 to 8 hr.
Note: This recipe requires a slow cooker.

4	veal loin chops, 6–8 oz (175–250 g) each
4	lamb chops, 4–6 oz (175–250 g) each
3 cans (8 oz/227 g)	Hunt's tomato sauce
½ cup (125 mL)	freshly grated Parmesan cheese

1. In a large frying pan over medium heat, in batches, brown veal and lamb chops for 2 minutes on each side and then place in the slow cooker.

2. Pour tomato sauce over chops in the slow cooker. Cook on Low for 6 to 8 hours or on High for 4 hours. Meat should be fork-tender. Remove meat from bones and discard bones. Stir in Parmesan and serve.

VARIATION

Use pork chops in place of veal and/or lamb chops.

NUTRITION STATS   per ¹/₁₀ recipe

Calories 290;   **Fat** 16 g;   **Sodium** 510 mg;   **Carbs** 7 g;   **Fibre** 2 g;   **Protein** 27 g

Spezza's Shoot-Out Sea Bass

Serves: 1
Prep: 5 min.
Bake: 8 to 10 min.

Fish is performance *and* brain food. When the crunch is on in a shoot-out, pull your best moves to deke out the goalie. Jennifer Spezza says their kids love this dish, and she makes it every week.

1	sea bass fillet (about 6–8 oz/175–250 g)
	Salt and pepper
1 cup (250 mL)	thinly sliced fennel
1 clove	garlic, thinly sliced
1	lemon or orange, sliced with peel
2 tbsp (30 mL)	white wine (optional)

1. Preheat oven to 375°F (190°C).

2. Season fish with salt and pepper to taste.

3. Place fennel in a small glass baking dish or casserole dish. Place fish on bed of fennel and top with garlic and lemon slices. Drizzle with white wine (if using). Bake for 8 to 10 minutes or until fish is tender and flakes easily with a fork.

NUTRITION STATS *per 1 recipe*
Calories 350; **Fat** 4.5 g; **Sodium** 570 mg; **Carbs** 33 g; **Fibre** 10 g; **Protein** 40 g

Jason with his wife, Jennifer, and daughters, Nicola and Sophia.

Jason Spezza

Born: Mississauga, ON

Played: Ottawa, Dallas

Fact: Jason likes to pair this fish dish with PASS Salad (page 139). His wife, Jennifer, uses any leftovers to make fish cakes for the kids.

9 Crazy for Quinoa

Quinoa is an über healthy and versatile superfood, and it's not just for vegetarians and those on a wheat-free diet—it's a great choice for athletes looking for something quick, simple, and packed with carbs, fibre, and protein. Because quinoa has a neutral taste, it soaks up whatever flavour it is paired with, and you can add it to almost everything, including Sniper Smoothies (pages 60–81) and salads. We love quinoa so much we wanted to share some of our easy, delicious creations.

Quinoa: Ultimate Protein

Quinoa (*keen-wah*) is actually a seed (also called a grain) that belongs to the spinach and chard family. It contains every amino acid, which makes it a complete protein. It's also a very good source of lysine, which aids in muscle repair, is rich in B vitamins, and is a good source of fibre.

Because it is a complete protein, quinoa is the perfect fuel for athletes, and many players consume it on a daily basis. It's a great substitute for energy-zapping pasta and bread that can spike blood sugar levels. Experiment going gluten-free on a few key days, and you'll see and feel the difference in performance.

Cooked quinoa can be stored in an airtight container in the refrigerator for up to 3 days. Make double batches weekly (see recipe below) and freeze extras for up to 1 month. Simply defrost and use for Quinoa Bowls (pages 232–239), Quinoa Net-Stuffing Peppers (page 248), Centre-Ice Qui'nana Smoothie (page 73), and RJ's Gold-Medal Pre-Game Quinoa with Chicken (page 237). For more on quinoa, see From the Pros by Kathy Smart (page 172).

How to Cook Quinoa

1 cup (250 mL)	quinoa, rinsed and drained
1½ cups (375 mL)	water or reduced-sodium broth (vegetable, chicken, beef)

Makes: 3 cups (750 mL)
Prep: 5 min.
Cook: 15 min.

1. Quinoa seeds have a naturally bitter coating, so either purchase pre-rinsed quinoa (check the label) or place the quinoa in a fine-mesh sieve and rinse under cold running water for about 1 minute or until the water runs clear.

2. In a medium saucepan over high heat, combine quinoa and water, cover, and bring to a boil. Reduce the heat to low and simmer for 12 minutes. Remove from heat (keep covered) and let stand for 5 minutes or until all water is absorbed and air holes appear on surface of quinoa. Fluff with a fork and either enjoy immediately or store for future meals (see above).

Tips Cooked quinoa almost looks like it is sprouted, with the inner seed separating from the outer layer, which looks like a circle.

Quinoa can be cooked in a rice cooker just as you would rice.

NUTRITION STATS   *per 1 cup* (250 mL)

Calories 222;   **Fat** 3.4 g;   **Sodium** 13 mg;   **Carbs** 39 g;   **Fibre** 5 g;   **Protein** 8.14 g

Rebecca with her mom, Colleen.

Rebecca Johnston

Born: Sudbury, ON

Played: Team Canada (gold medallist 2010, 2014)

Fact: Rebecca likes to eat this quinoa dish for lunch or as a quick afternoon snack while training. It's very nutritious and contains a lot of protein.

RJ's Gold-Medal Pre-Game Quinoa with Chicken

Rebecca likes to eat this dish about 4 hours before games. Given the stack of medals she has earned, it's clearly a winner.

Makes: *4 cups (1 L)*
Prep: *15 min.*
Cook: *20 min.*

2 cups (500 mL)	water
2 cubes	chicken bouillon
1 clove	garlic, smashed
1 cup (250 mL)	quinoa, rinsed and drained
2	cooked large boneless, skinless chicken breasts, cut into bite-size pieces
1	large red onion, diced
1	large green pepper, diced
½ cup (125 mL)	chopped Kalamata olives
½ cup (125 mL)	crumbled feta cheese
¼ cup (60 mL)	chopped fresh parsley leaves
¼ cup (60 mL)	chopped fresh chives
	Sea salt
1 cup (250 mL)	Balsamic Winger-grette Dressing (page 150)

1. In a saucepan over medium-high heat, bring water, bouillon, and garlic to a boil. Stir in quinoa, reduce heat to medium-low, and cover. Simmer for 15 to 20 minutes or until quinoa is tender and water has been absorbed. Discard garlic clove and spoon quinoa into a large bowl.

2. To quinoa, add chicken, onion, green pepper, olives, feta, parsley, and chives, season with salt to taste, and gently combine. Drizzle with dressing and stir until evenly combined. Serve warm or refrigerate for 2 hours and serve cold.

NUTRITION STATS *per ⅙ recipe*
(using regular chicken bouillon)

Calories 450; **Fat** 26 g; **Sodium** 610 mg; **Carbs** 28 g; **Fibre** 3 g; **Protein** 27 g

Erin's Quinoa Bowl

Serves: 2
Prep: 10 min.
Cook: 0

Erin is the queen of assembling amazing ingredients in a bowl in minutes. The key is having cooked and prepped ingredients in your fridge. Be creative in deciding what goes into your player's bowl.

1 cup (250 mL)	shredded lettuce
½ cup (125 mL)	cooked quinoa
½ cup (125 mL)	diced cooked chicken, beef, or shrimp
¼ cup (60 mL)	Bench-Clearing Bean Dip (page 132)
¼ cup (60 mL)	diced cucumber
2 tbsp (30 mL)	fresh or frozen corn
1 tbsp (15 mL)	alfalfa sprouts
1 tbsp (15 mL)	crumbled feta cheese
1 tbsp (15 mL)	minced fresh herbs (coriander, parsley, basil)
3 tbsp (45 mL)	Clutch Caesar Dressing (page 146) or Balsamic Winger-grette Dressing (page 150)

1. Following the order listed, layer ingredients in a large bowl, with dressing drizzled over top.

NUTRITION STATS   *per ½ recipe*

Calories 250;   **Fat** 12 g;   **Sodium** 260 mg;   **Carbs** 17.5 g;   **Fibre** 3.5 g;   **Protein** 18 g

Korey's Quinoa Bowl

Always having cooked quinoa on hand makes for a 5-minute meal that can be switched up by using different sauces and toppings. Korey loves this pesto-spinach combo, with tomatoes adding a splash of colour.

Serves: 2
Prep: 5 min.
Cook: 2 min.

2 cups (500 mL)	fresh spinach leaves
1 cup (250 mL)	cooked quinoa
¼ cup (60 mL)	basil pesto
2 tbsp (30 mL)	no-salt-added diced tomatoes

1. In a large bowl, combine spinach and quinoa and microwave on High for 2 minutes.

2. Top with pesto and tomatoes and stir.

NUTRITION STATS   *per ½ recipe*

Calories 245;   **Fat** 14.5 g;   **Sodium** 130 mg;   **Carbs** 23 g;   **Fibre** 4 g;   **Protein** 6 g

Speedy Salade Quin'oise

Serves: 4 to 6 people
Prep: 20 min.
Cook: 15 min.

Quinoa replaces the potatoes traditionally used in the inspiration for this salad, salade niçoise. As an easily digested complete protein with slow-release carbs, the quinoa makes this dish a top-shelf pre-game meal. Having ready-made ingredients—quinoa, hard-boiled eggs, and salad dressing—on hand speeds up recipe assembly.

2 cups (500 mL)	cooked quinoa
1 cup (250 mL)	trimmed green beans, blanched and halved
¾ cup (175 mL)	cherry or grape tomatoes, halved
¼ cup (60 mL)	sliced red onion
3	hard-boiled large eggs, peeled and halved
¼ cup (60 mL)	niçoise or pitted Kalamata olives
½ cup (125 mL)	extra virgin olive oil
¼ cup (60 mL)	red wine vinegar
1 tbsp (15 mL)	Dijon mustard
1 tbsp (15 mL)	minced fresh herbs (parsley, chives, and/or basil)
½ tsp (2.5 mL)	granulated sugar
	Salt and pepper
6 to 8 oz (175 to 250 g)	grilled rainbow trout or chicken breast (optional)

1. Place quinoa in centre of a shallow serving bowl. Surround with green beans, tomatoes, and red onion. Arrange eggs around perimeter of bowl and top with olives.

2. In a small bowl, whisk together oil, vinegar, mustard, herbs, and sugar. Season with salt and pepper to taste. Set aside. (Dressing can be prepared 24 hours in advance and refrigerated.)

3. Just before serving, drizzle salad with dressing and top with grilled fish or chicken (if using).

VARIATION

Use Balsamic Winger-grette Dressing (page 150) or Clutch Caesar Dressing (page 146) instead of this vinaigrette.

NUTRITION STATS *per ⅙ recipe*

Calories 345; **Fat** 25 g; **Sodium** 153 mg; **Carbs** 17 g; **Fibre** 2.7 g; **Protein** 13 g

Asian Quinoa Bowl

The Asian dressing gives this bowl a distinctive and satisfying flavour. Add whatever veggies you love—asparagus and broccoli would be amazing, too.

Serves: 2
Prep: 5 min.
Cook: 2 to 3 min.

1 cup (250 mL)	cooked quinoa
1 cup (250 mL)	finely chopped bok choy
¼ cup (60 mL)	grated carrots
2 tbsp (30 mL)	Visor-Foggin' Asian Dressing (page 153)
2 tbsp (30 mL)	minced green onions

1. In a large bowl, combine quinoa, bok choy, and carrots and microwave on High for 2 to 3 minutes or until bok choy and carrots are tender.

2. Drizzle with dressing, stir, and top with green onions.

NUTRITION STATS   *per ½ recipe*

Calories 180;   **Fat** 7 g;   **Sodium** 210 mg;   **Carbs** 25 g;   **Fibre** 4 g;   **Protein** 6 g

Italian Quinoa Bowl

Fresh basil, tomatoes, and Parmesan never tasted so good in such a healthful way! Make your own pesto or use a high-quality brand. Or try a generous spoonful of minced basil leaves for a fresh-herb version.

Serves: 2
Prep: 5 min.
Cook: 2 to 3 min.

1 cup (250 mL)	cooked quinoa
1 cup (250 mL)	fresh baby spinach leaves
½ cup (125 mL)	reduced-sodium tomato sauce
2 tbsp (30 mL)	basil pesto (optional)
1 tbsp (15 mL)	freshly grated Parmesan cheese (optional)

1. In a large bowl, combine quinoa, spinach, and tomato sauce and microwave on High for 2 to 3 minutes or until hot.

2. Stir and top with pesto and Parmesan.

Tip *Try topping with Alfie's Power Play Meat Sauce (page 204), as shown in the photo.*

NUTRITION STATS   *per ½ recipe*
(using no-salt-added tomato sauce)

Calories 210;   **Fat** 8.5 g;   **Sodium** 100 mg;   **Carbs** 27 g;   **Fibre** 5 g;   **Protein** 6 g

Mexican Quinoa Bowl

Serves: 2
Prep: 5 min.
Cook: 0

Quickly assemble the flavours of Mexico in a quinoa bowl! Use store-bought salsa and guacamole or make your own (see pages 232–249).

1 cup (250 mL)	chopped romaine or iceberg lettuce (optional)
1 cup (250 mL)	cooked quinoa
¼ cup (60 mL)	Heatley's Light the Lamp Salsa (page 131)
¼ cup (60 mL)	sliced avocado or Redden's Rippin' Guacamole (page 128)
2 tbsp (30 mL)	finely chopped green onions
1 tbsp (15 mL)	chopped fresh cilantro leaves (optional)
	Hot sauce, to taste
	Yorky's Checking Chicken Taco filling (optional, page 196)

1. Following the order listed, layer ingredients in a large serving bowl.

NUTRITION STATS   *per ½ recipe*
Calories 165;   **Fat** 5.5 g;   **Sodium** 53 mg;   **Carbs** 25 g;   **Fibre** 5 g;   **Protein** 6 g

Mediterranean Quinoa Bowl

Look for gluten-free, store-bought tabbouleh or make your own. If you use quinoa instead of bulgur, you can turn this into an all-quinoa dish. Bowls offer a refreshing change from sandwiches and wraps.

Serves: 2
Prep: 5 min.
Cook: 0

1 cup (250 mL)	cooked quinoa
½ cup (125 mL)	shredded romaine or iceberg lettuce (optional)
¼ cup (60 mL)	tabbouleh
2 tbsp (30 mL)	Quick-Hands Hummus (page 123)
2 tbsp (30 mL)	diced tomatoes and/or cucumbers
1 tbsp (15 mL)	Kalamata olives or crumbled feta (optional)

1. Following the order listed, layer ingredients in a large serving bowl.

NUTRITION STATS *per 1 recipe*

Calories 165; **Fat** 5 g; **Sodium** 115 mg; **Carbs** 25 g; **Fibre** 4.5 g; **Protein** 5.5 g

Quinoa Net-Stuffing Peppers

Serves: 6 to 8
Prep: 30 min.
Cook: 1 hr. 16 min.
Stand: 5 min.

The quinoa in the filling provides whole-grain goodness and a serving of protein—all the better to stuff the net (score a goal).

2 tbsp (30 mL)	coconut oil or olive oil
1 cup (250 mL)	finely chopped onion
½ cup (125 mL)	finely chopped celery
1 tbsp (15 mL)	ground cumin
2 cloves	garlic, minced
1 package (10 oz/283 g)	frozen chopped spinach, thawed and squeezed dry
2 cans (15 oz/398 mL)	diced tomatoes, drained, liquid reserved
1 can (19 oz/540 mL)	black beans, rinsed and drained, or 2 cups (500 mL) Bench-Clearing Bean Dip (page 132)
¾ cup (175 mL)	quinoa, rinsed and drained
1½ cups (375 mL)	grated carrots
2 cups (500 mL)	water
1½ cups (375 mL)	shredded reduced-fat pepper Jack cheese, divided
4	large red peppers, halved lengthwise, ribs removed

Tips *To make soup: Chop up leftover stuffed peppers, add to saucepan with 2 cups (500 mL) broth (your choice of flavour), and simmer until soup is hot.*

Simplify and speed up prep: Stuff peppers with a mixture of cooked quinoa, Bench-Clearing Bean Dip (page 132), and cheese, then bake according to recipe directions.

1. Preheat oven to 350°F (180°C). In the bottom of a 13- by 9-inch (33 by 23 cm) glass baking dish, pour liquid from canned tomatoes.

2. In a saucepan over medium heat, heat oil. Add onion and celery, and cook for 5 minutes or until soft. Add cumin and garlic, and sauté for 1 minute. Stir in spinach and drained tomatoes. Cook for 5 minutes or until most liquid evaporates. Stir in black beans, quinoa, carrots, and water. Cover and bring to a boil. Reduce heat to medium-low and simmer for 20 minutes or until quinoa is tender. Stir in 1 cup (250 mL) cheese.

3. Fill each pepper half with heaping ¾ cup (175 mL) quinoa mixture, and place in baking dish. Cover with foil. Bake for 1 hour. Uncover and sprinkle each pepper with 1 tbsp (15 mL) remaining cheese. Bake for

15 minutes more or until cheese is melted and tops of stuffed peppers are browned. Let stand for 5 minutes.

4. Transfer stuffed peppers to serving plates and drizzle each with pan juices before serving.

NUTRITION STATS   *per 1 stuffed pepper* (½ pepper)

Calories 240;   **Fat** 9 g;   **Sodium** 370 mg;   **Carbs** 28 g;   **Fibre** 10 g;   **Protein** 13 g

Sin Bin

We can't deny it: desserts make everyone happy. That being said, indulging in them can trigger crashing energy levels and tempt the player to reach, trip, and slash while trying to keep up. When the carbs we eat contain simple sugars and are highly processed—as they are in most desserts—we digest them very quickly and they enter the blood rapidly. Our body reacts with a huge release of insulin in an attempt to lower the level of glucose (sugar) in the blood: the "rush." Afterwards we are left with low blood sugar (hypoglycemia) and feel hungry and tired: the "crash." Avoid being thrown into the sin bin (penalty box) by enjoying these treats in moderation on your off days.

Coach's Wheelin' Peanut Butter and Banana Cookies

Makes: 36
Prep: 15 min.
Bake: 15 to 18 min.

Coach Tracey, former women's Wisconsin Badger's assistant hockey coach, says this is a fan and family favourite and keeps her players wheelin' (skating with great speed and puck control). Gobble them up while they are still warm!

3	ripe bananas, mashed
1 tbsp (15 mL)	pure vanilla extract
¾ cup (175 mL)	natural smooth or chunky peanut butter
3 tbsp (45 mL)	pure maple syrup
2½ cups (625 mL)	large-flake rolled oats
½ cup (125 mL)	whole-wheat flour
1 tsp (5 mL)	baking powder
¼ tsp (1 mL)	salt (optional)
½ cup (125 mL)	non-dairy chocolate chips or raisins or both

1. Preheat oven to 350°F (180°C). Line a baking sheet with parchment paper.

2. In a large bowl, using an electric mixer on high speed, mix bananas, vanilla, peanut butter, and maple syrup until creamy.

3. In a medium bowl, combine oats, flour, baking powder, and salt (if using). Add to wet ingredients and stir until well combined (the batter should be slightly sticky). Fold in chocolate chips.

4. Drop 1 tbsp (15 mL) mounds of dough spaced evenly apart onto prepared baking sheet. Bake on middle rack of oven for 15 to 18 minutes or until golden and firm to the touch. Cool on baking sheet for 5 minutes and then turn out onto a wire rack to cool completely. Store for up to 3 days in an airtight container, but these are best right out of the oven.

Variation

To make this dessert gluten-free, substitute an equal amount of gluten-free flour or quinoa flakes for the whole-wheat flour and choose gluten-free rolled oats.

Tips *You can also use frozen bananas. Microwave them on High for 1½ minutes or until just thawed. Drain off the liquid, mash, and follow recipe instructions.*

To boost the nutrition factor, add 2 to 3 tbsp (30 to 45 mL) flaxseeds and sub in raw cacao nibs for the chocolate chips.

Freeze heaping 1 tbsp (15 mL) mounds of batter on a parchment-lined tray for 40 minutes or until solid enough to transfer to an airtight storage container. For hot cookies on demand, take out as many frozen portions as you need. Add 2 minutes to the baking time.

NUTRITION STATS *per 1 cookie (20 g)*

Calories 60; **Fat** 2 g; **Sodium** 20 mg; **Carbs** 10 g; **Fibre** 1 g; **Protein** 2 g

Peanut Butter

Kids love peanut butter, and so do we. We love it for its simplicity and its nutritional value: 2 tbsp (30 mL) of peanut butter contain 7 g of protein, which is why it's a great way to start off the day. This protein also helps build and repair muscles, which makes it a smart snack for when players step off the ice. And 2 tbsp (30 mL) is the perfect serving size to deliver the health benefits but not overdo the fats and sugar.

Besides protein, peanut butter is rich in fibre, healthy fats, iron, potassium, antioxidants, magnesium, and more. A big worry is that it is high in fats—this is somewhat true, but it is higher in unsaturated fats (or good fats) than saturated fats, which we know are essential to our bodies.

An even healthier option is natural peanut butter, which has less additives and lacks the palm oil found in most mass-market peanut butter. Palm oil is an unhealthy oil used to prevent oil separation, which tends to be the worst complaint of natural peanut butter. But there is a simple solution: stir! Store natural peanut butter in the fridge because it doesn't have as long a shelf life as mass-market peanut butter.

Soy nut butter—a peanut butter substitute that was created for people with allergies to peanuts and tree nuts—is also a great option. It is school-safe and is pretty comparable as far as nutrition goes: soy butter has about the same amount of protein, less fat, more carbs, and a bit less of the vitamin spectrum but overall is a healthy substitute.

Check out Knock-Down Nibbles (pages 114–119) for Pucks on a Bench (page 111), Banana Backhanders (page 113), Power Pucks (page 114), and Chewy Bar-Downs (page 118), and don't forget about our Stanley's PB-Cup Smoothie (page 78), found in Sniper Smoothies (pages 60–81)!

Peanut Butter Paddles

The paddle (goalie stick) may miss a few shots while dreaming about these yummy cookies. Traditional peanut butter cookies get a healthy lift with chia seeds, which add omega-3 fatty acids, fibre, and crunch.

Makes: 24 cookies
Prep: 5 min.
Bake: 10 min.
Cool: 10 min.

1 cup (250 mL)	creamy peanut butter
½ cup (125 mL)	lightly packed light brown sugar
1	large egg
2 tbsp (30 mL)	whole chia seeds

1. Preheat oven to 325°F (160°C). Line a baking sheet with parchment paper.

2. In a medium bowl, combine all of the ingredients until smooth.

3. Place 1 tbsp (15 mL) mounds of dough onto prepared baking sheet. Bake on middle rack of oven for 10 minutes or until cookies are browned. Remove from oven and let cool for 10 minutes on baking sheet and then set on wire rack to cool completely. Store for up to 3 days in an airtight container, but these are best right out of the oven.

Tip For a school-safe snack, substitute soy or sunflower butter for the peanut butter.

NUTRITION STATS *per 1 cookie (15 g)*

Calories 80; **Fat** 5 g; **Sodium** 0 mg; **Carbs** 6 g; **Fibre** 1 g; **Protein** 3 g

Richardson's Buckeyes

Makes: 24 cookies
Prep: 15 min.
Bake: 0
Chill: 90 min.

These peanut butter balls are a popular treat in Columbus, Ohio, where Luke played for the Columbus Blue Jackets and coached his daughters, Morgan and Daron, in hockey—and the girls love them, too. The name comes from the Ohio State Buckeyes, the official name of the university's sports teams. A buckeye is a nut and a symbol of good luck.

¾ cup (175 mL)	butter, softened
1½ cups (375 mL)	sifted confectioners' (icing) sugar
1 cup (250 mL)	creamy peanut butter
1 tbsp (15 mL)	2% milk
½ tsp (2.5 mL)	pure vanilla extract
16 oz (454 g)	semisweet chocolate
1 tbsp (15 mL)	shortening

1. Line a baking sheet with parchment paper.

2. In a medium bowl, using an electric mixer on medium-high speed, cream butter and sugar until smooth. Add peanut butter and beat until smooth. Mix in milk and vanilla until well combined and not sticky. If dough is not firm enough, mix in additional sugar 1 tbsp (15 mL) at a time until dough can be rolled by hand. Cover and refrigerate for 30 minutes.

3. Using your hands, roll dough into 1-inch (2.5 cm) balls and place onto prepared baking sheet. Refrigerate for at least 30 minutes.

4. In a small saucepan over low heat, melt chocolate and shortening.

5. Remove dough balls from fridge. Press your finger or the rounded end of a small stick into a ball, then dip three-quarters of the ball into the chocolate. Place it on the baking sheet, hole-side up. Repeat for all of the balls. Refrigerate for at least 30 minutes or until chocolate is hardened.

Tips Add crunch by gently rolling these in crushed unsalted peanuts after dipping in melted chocolate.

These will keep in an airtight container in the fridge for up to 1 week.

NUTRITION STATS *per 1 cookie* (15 g)
Calories 80; **Fat** 6 g; **Sodium** 15 mg; **Carbs** 7 g; **Fibre** 1 g; **Protein** 1 g

Luke with his daughters, Daron and Morgan.

Luke Richardson

Born: Ottawa, ON

Played: Toronto, Edmonton, Philadelphia, Tampa, Ottawa

Fact: This recipe, shared by Luke's mother-in-law, is a Richardson family favourite. It's a great treat to share at tournaments.

Liam's Chocolate Chippies

Makes: 48 cookies
Prep: 10 min.
Bake: 12 to 16 min.

These cookies are a favourite of Korey's husband, Liam. Word is he may become somewhat chippie (physical and aggressive play) if someone takes his chocolate chip cookies—not really, but we tease him! Make a double batch of dough: one to bake and enjoy immediately and one to freeze as ready-to-bake dough balls.

1 cup (250 mL)	butter, softened
¾ cup (175 mL)	lightly packed light brown sugar
¾ cup (175 mL)	granulated sugar
1	large egg
2¼ cups (550 mL)	all-purpose flour
1 tsp (5 mL)	baking powder
1 tsp (5 mL)	baking soda
2 cups (500 mL)	semisweet chocolate chips

1. Preheat oven to 375°F (190°C). Line a baking sheet with parchment paper.

2. In a large bowl, using a hand mixer on medium-high speed, cream together butter and sugars until light and fluffy. Add egg and beat on high speed for 1 minute. Add flour, baking powder, and baking soda and stir until just combined. Fold in chocolate chips.

3. Place heaping 1 tbsp (15 mL) mounds of dough onto prepared baking sheet. Bake on middle rack of oven for 10 to 12 minutes or until golden and firm to touch. Cool for 5 minutes on baking sheet and then turn out onto a wire rack to cool completely. Store in an airtight container for up to 3 days, but these are best right out of the oven.

MAKE-AHEAD

You can freeze this cookie dough for on-demand cookies. Form the dough into balls and then freeze on a baking sheet. Once the balls are firm, you can transfer them to an airtight container. To bake from frozen, just pull out the amount you need and bake as usual, adding a couple minutes to the baking time.

NUTRITION STATS *per 1 cookie (20 g)*

Calories 140; **Fat** 7 g; **Sodium** 170 mg; **Carbs** 20 g; **Fibre** 1 g; **Protein** 2 g

Spezza Pie

Serves: 8
Prep: 20 min.
Bake: 30 min.
Cool: 20 min.

No need for a rolling pin to enjoy pie! Jennifer Spezza cuts a double-crust recipe in half and then makes a crumble topping instead of a crust—a smart idea that reduces calories without sacrificing the comfort-food appeal of this traditional fruit pairing.

Crumble pie topping

1⅓ cups (325 mL)	all-purpose flour
½ tsp (2.5 mL)	sea salt
⅓ cup (75 mL)	vegetable oil
3 tbsp (45 mL)	cold 2% milk

Filling

1¼ cups (300 mL)	granulated sugar
⅓ cup (75 mL)	all-purpose flour
¼ tsp (1 mL)	ground nutmeg
¼ tsp (1 mL)	ground cinnamon
3 cups (750 mL)	halved fresh strawberries
2 cups (500 mL)	thinly sliced rhubarb
2 tbsp (30 mL)	cold butter, cut into small pieces

1. Preheat oven to 400°F (200°C)

2. **Make topping:** In a medium bowl, combine flour and salt. Make a well in the middle.

3. In a measuring cup, combine oil and milk. Pour into well in dry ingredients. Using a fork, stir until mixture becomes soft and crumbly. Refrigerate until ready to use.

4. **Make filling:** In a large bowl, combine sugar, flour, nutmeg, and cinnamon. Add strawberries and rhubarb, and gently stir to coat well.

5. Pour filling into an 8-inch (20 cm) square metal baking pan. Scatter pieces of butter on top. Sprinkle crumble topping evenly over filling. Bake on middle rack of oven for 30 minutes or until rhubarb is tender and topping is browned. Remove from oven and set aside to cool for 20 minutes before serving.

Jason with his wife, Jennifer, and daughters, Nicola and Sophia.

Jason Spezza

Born: Mississauga, ON

Played: Ottawa, Dallas

Fact: This dessert is a Spezza family holiday tradition—a little after-dinner indulgence enjoyed with a scoop of vanilla ice cream.

NUTRITION STATS   *per ⅛ recipe*

Calories 345;   **Fat** 13 g;   **Sodium** 27 mg;   **Carbs** 55 g;   **Fibre** 3 g;   **Protein** 4.8 g

Winning Apple Crisp

There is nothing like coming home to the smell of apples and cinnamon, especially after getting a couple of apples (assists) to win the game! Celebrate and please the taste buds with this fruit-full dessert topped with fibre-rich oats and cinnamon. Not just for dessert—it makes a great breakfast, too.

Serves: 6 to 8
Prep: 10 min.
Bake: 30 to 40 min.

1 cup (250 mL)	quick-cooking or large-flake rolled oats (look for gluten-free)
⅓ cup (75 mL)	whole-wheat flour
½ cup (125 mL)	lightly packed brown sugar, divided
1 tsp (5 mL)	ground cinnamon, divided
⅓ cup (75 mL)	unsweetened apple juice, divided
3 tbsp (45 mL)	butter, melted
6	apples, peeled, cored, and thinly sliced
1 tbsp (15 mL)	freshly squeezed lemon juice

1. Preheat oven to 375°F (190°C). Grease an 8-inch (20 cm) square glass baking dish.

2. In a medium bowl, combine oats, flour, ⅓ cup (75 mL) brown sugar, and ½ tsp (2.5 mL) cinnamon. Stir in 2½ tbsp (37 mL) apple juice and all of the butter. Set aside.

3. In prepared baking dish, combine apples, lemon juice, remaining apple juice, remaining brown sugar, and remaining cinnamon. Sprinkle oatmeal mixture evenly over apples. Bake in oven for 30 to 40 minutes or until apples are tender and topping is golden brown.

Tip *Make 6 individual servings using 1-cup (250 mL) ramekins. Divide filling and topping evenly among the ramekins, and bake for 30 minutes or until apples are tender and topping is golden brown.*

NUTRITION STATS *per ⅛ recipe*

Calories 250; **Fat** 6 g; **Sodium** 40 mg; **Carbs** 49 g; **Fibre** 5 g; **Protein** 4 g

Dan Boyle's Yummy Hat Trick

Serves: 15
Prep: 30 min.
Bake: 15 min.
Cool: 12 hr.

Family traditions go a long way when players are on the road away from family for long periods. It's mealtimes and togetherness that they most often reminisce and look forward to. Desserts add a sense of celebration when a player is home, and this one guarantees sweet memories with not one or two creamy fillings but three—now that's a hat trick!

Crust

½ cup (125 mL)	butter
2 cups (500 mL)	graham cracker crumbs

Filling

8 oz (250 g)	cream cheese, softened
1 cup (250 mL)	confectioners' (icing) sugar
1 cup (250 mL)	35% whipping cream
1 package (3.9 oz/110 g)	instant chocolate pudding
1 package (3.9 oz/110 g)	instant vanilla pudding
3 cups (750 mL)	milk, divided

1. Preheat oven to 350°F (180°C).

2. In a small saucepan over medium heat, melt butter. Remove from heat and stir in cracker crumbs.

3. Press crumbs into a 13- by 9-inch (33 by 23 cm) metal baking pan. Bake in oven for 10 minutes or until golden brown. Set aside to cool completely.

4. Meanwhile, in a medium bowl, using an electric mixer on medium-high speed, beat cream cheese and sugar together until smooth. Spread over cooled base in baking pan.

5. In a separate medium bowl, using an electric mixer on medium-high speed, whip cream until stiff peaks form. Spread half of the beaten cream over the cream cheese layer in baking pan.

6. In a separate medium bowl, using an electric mixer on medium-high speed, beat together chocolate pudding mix and 1½ cups (375 mL)

Dan with his mom, Diane.

Dan Boyle

Born: Ottawa, ON

Played: Florida, Tampa, San Jose, New York

Fact: This family recipe was passed down by Dan's grandma. It's become a favourite holiday dessert when the entire Boyle clan gets together at Christmastime.

milk for 2 minutes or until pudding has thickened. Pour over whipped-cream layer in baking pan.

7. In a separate medium bowl, using an electric mixer on medium-high speed, beat together vanilla pudding mix with remaining 1½ cups (375 mL) milk for 2 minutes or until pudding had thickened. Pour over chocolate pudding layer in baking pan.

8. Top with remaining whipped cream. Chill for at least 12 hours or overnight.

NUTRITION STATS *per ¹/₁₅ recipe*

Calories 310; **Fat** 19 g; **Sodium** 400 mg; **Carbs** 32 g; **Fibre** 1 g; **Protein** 4 g

Zdeno Chára's Rocket Rice Pudding

Serves: 8 to 10
Prep: 15 min.
Cook: 1 hr. 30 min.

Lots of love goes into making this nutritious rice pudding, which is baked in a pan with added fruit. It's Zdeno's favourite dessert and helps fuel his rocket of a shot.

1¾ cup (425 mL)	arborio rice, rinsed and drained
4 cups (1 L)	2% milk
2 pinches	salt
1 tbsp (15 mL)	butter, softened
¼ cup (60 mL)	dried bread crumbs
3	eggs, separated
½ cup (125 mL)	butter, softened
½ cup (125 mL)	granulated sugar
¼ cup (60 mL)	raisins or dried unsweetened cranberries
2 cans (15 oz/425 g each)	apricots, peaches, or other fruit, strained

Zdeno with his wife, Tatiana.

Zdeno Chára

Born: Trenčín, Slovakia

Played: New York, Ottawa, Boston

Fact: Chara eats half of Tatiana's recipe one day and the other half the following day!

1. In a medium saucepan over medium heat, combine rice, milk, and salt and bring to a light boil. Reduce heat to low and simmer, covered, for 25 to 30 minutes, stirring often to prevent burning, until milk is absorbed and rice is tender. Remove from heat and set aside to cool completely.

2. Preheat oven to 350°F (180°C). Lightly grease a 13- by 9-inch (33 by 23 cm) glass baking dish with butter and sprinkle with bread crumbs to cover the entire dish (discard any bread crumbs that do not stick).

3. In a medium bowl, using an electric mixer on medium-high speed, beat egg whites to soft peaks.

4. In a large bowl, beat butter and sugar until light and fluffy. Gradually mix in egg yolks until mixture is light yellow. Add cooled rice mixture to egg mixture and stir well. Gently stir in egg whites. Add raisins and stir until just incorporated. Pour half of the rice mixture into the greased casserole and spread evenly using a spatula. Neatly top with a layer of apricots, then carefully spread remaining rice mixture over top. Bake in oven for 1 hour. Remove from oven and set aside for 20 minutes to cool.

NUTRITION STATS *per ¹/₁₀ recipe*

Calories 390; **Fat** 14 g; **Sodium** 180 mg; **Carbs** 58 g; **Fibre** 1 g; **Protein** 8 g

ULTIMATE APPENDICES

FROM THE PROS

Tournament Life 101

Stephanie Richardson, the ultimate hockey mom to daughters Daron and Morgan and wife to ex-NHL-er Luke Richardson, is the master of tournament food and packing for the road. Here Stephanie shares her tips and tricks for keeping tournament life organized and healthy. (See also Stephanie Richardson's ideal tournament potluck meals on page 278.)

www.difd.com

We encourage parents and players to check out the Richardsons' Foundation and continue the conversations.

- Make sure your freezer packs are frozen and ready to go. Have a surplus on hand.

- Purchase hot packs so you can have hot meals on the road (you can find hot packs in different sizes in the camping sections of larger stores; you either boil or microwave them to get them hot). For example, cook a lasagna to eat on the way. Line individual serving containers with spinach leaves and top with a piece of lasagna (the spinach wilts and tastes yummy) and add some fresh broccoli on the side (it is warmed slightly by the hot lasagna), then place the containers in the insulated bag and top with hot packs. Hours down the road you'll have a warm, healthy meal.

- There are more uses for Red Solo cups than adults think! Use them to serve yogurt parfaits, veggies and dip, smoothies, and, of course, beer and wine for the parents!

- Smoothies make great, healthy snacks. Pack Greek yogurt and frozen berries (frozen berries keep longer) and remember to bring your blender, protein powder, and supplements.

- Make up individual servings of carrot and celery sticks in snack-size resealable bags. Along with an apple, they're a great grab-and-go snack to tide you over until mealtime.

- Pack hard-boiled and peeled eggs to add protein to meals. Cooked chickpeas also work well (add them to salads!).

- Always bring along the following to supplement meals and/or for snacking: almonds, microwave popcorn, oatmeal (see page 95) and maple syrup, and raisins.

- For meals on the road, combine whole-wheat rigatoni, raw broccoli and peppers, and cooked cubed chicken breasts tossed in a light pesto sauce. It will keep for the whole weekend, and you can eat it hot or cold. Store it in individual-size resealable containers so it's easy to grab and eat in the hotel or the car. Another great option is quinoa salad with spinach leaves, strips of sweet pepper, crumbled feta cheese, a drizzle of olive oil and a pinch of black pepper.

COOLER AND TRAVEL NECESSITIES

- Bottle/wine opener
- Dish soap
- Blender
- Paper towels
- Plastic cutlery
- Red Solo cups
- Small cutting board
- Sharp knife

TOURNAMENT MEAL PLANNING

There are many variables to consider when planning a tournament: timing of games, distance from hotel to arena, available meeting rooms for team potlucks, timing of pre-game and post-game snacks and meals. Taking the time to plan appropriately can simplify meals and reduce the heavy expenses of eating out as well as provide more time for team-bonding activities. See pages 272–278 for some templates to get you started. Go to www.hockeyfood.com for downloadable copies of the meal plans.

Go to www.hockeyfood.com for a downloadable copy of this chart.

TOURNAMENT MEAL-PLANNING TEMPLATES

Organizer: ______________________________

Team name: ______________________________

Dates: ______________________________

Hotel name: Phone #:

Hotel address:

Kitchen facilities: ☐ Yes ☐ No

Common room: ☐ Yes ☐ No

Restrictions:

Equipment available: ☐ Yes ☐ No What kind?

Team purchase extra hotel room for meals? ☐ Yes ☐ No

Restaurant in hotel? ☐ Yes ☐ No

Breakfast included? ☐ Yes ☐ No

Restaurants close by:

Grocery stores close to hotel (name and address):

1. Phone #:
2. Phone #:
3. Phone #:

TOURNAMENT DAY 1

Game 1 VS.   Start time:

Location of arena: Arrival time:

Pre-Game Meal   Eat as a team?   Meal location:
☐ Breakfast ☐ Lunch ☐ Dinner ☐ Snack   ☐ Yes ☐ No

Post-game recovery snack in change room: ☐ Chocolate milk ☐ Smoothie ☐ Oranges ☐ Apples

Time between games: Distance between arenas:

Post-Game Meal   Eat as a team?   Meal location:
☐ Breakfast ☐ Lunch ☐ Dinner ☐ Snack   ☐ Yes ☐ No

Game 2 VS.   Start time:

Location of arena: Arrival time:

Pre-Game Meal   Eat as a team?   Meal location:
☐ Breakfast ☐ Lunch ☐ Dinner ☐ Snack   ☐ Yes ☐ No

Post-game recovery snack in change room: ☐ Chocolate milk ☐ Smoothie ☐ Oranges ☐ Apples

Time between games: Distance between arenas:

Post-Game Meal   Eat as a team?   Meal location:
☐ Breakfast ☐ Lunch ☐ Dinner ☐ Snack   ☐ Yes ☐ No

Go to www.hockeyfood.com for a downloadable copy of this chart.

TOURNAMENT DAY 2

Game 1 VS.

Start time:

Location of arena:

Arrival time:

Pre-Game Meal

Eat as a team?

Meal location:

☐ Breakfast ☐ Lunch ☐ Dinner ☐ Snack

☐ Yes ☐ No

Post-game recovery snack in change room: ☐ Chocolate milk ☐ Smoothie ☐ Oranges ☐ Apples

Time between games:

Distance between arenas:

Post-Game Meal

Eat as a team?

Meal location:

☐ Breakfast ☐ Lunch ☐ Dinner ☐ Snack

☐ Yes ☐ No

Game 2 VS.

Start time:

Location of arena:

Arrival time:

Pre-Game Meal

Eat as a team?

Meal location:

☐ Breakfast ☐ Lunch ☐ Dinner ☐ Snack

☐ Yes ☐ No

Post-game recovery snack in change room: ☐ Chocolate milk ☐ Smoothie ☐ Oranges ☐ Apples

Time between games:

Distance between arenas:

Post-Game Meal

Eat as a team?

Meal location:

☐ Breakfast ☐ Lunch ☐ Dinner ☐ Snack

☐ Yes ☐ No

TOURNAMENT DAY 3

Game 1 VS.

Start time:

Location of arena:

Arrival time:

Pre-Game Meal

☐ Breakfast   ☐ Lunch   ☐ Dinner   ☐ Snack

Eat as a team?

☐ Yes   ☐ No

Meal location:

Post-game recovery snack in change room: ☐ Chocolate milk   ☐ Smoothie   ☐ Oranges   ☐ Apples

Time between games:

Distance between arenas:

Post-Game Meal

☐ Breakfast   ☐ Lunch   ☐ Dinner   ☐ Snack

Eat as a team?

☐ Yes   ☐ No

Meal location:

Game 2 VS.

Start time:

Location of arena:

Arrival time:

Pre-Game Meal

☐ Breakfast   ☐ Lunch   ☐ Dinner   ☐ Snack

Eat as a team?

☐ Yes   ☐ No

Meal location:

Post-game recovery snack in change room: ☐ Chocolate milk   ☐ Smoothie   ☐ Oranges   ☐ Apples

Time between games:

Distance between arenas:

Post-Game Meal

☐ Breakfast   ☐ Lunch   ☐ Dinner   ☐ Snack

Eat as a team?

☐ Yes   ☐ No

Meal location:

TEAM POTLUCK SIGN-UP SHEET

Coordinator: Number of people:

Theme: *Southwest Chicken Fajitas and Morning Banana Split Smoothies (recipes on www.hockeyfood.com)*

Meal Items	Player & Parent
Cooked and sliced chicken (7 lbs./3.25 kg) + slow cooker + serving tongs	1. 2.
Shredded cheese (2 lbs./1 kg) + serving dish and serving tongs	
Flour tortillas (45) + serving basket and serving tongs	
2 salsa + 2 bags tortilla chips + serving bowl and basket	
2 guacamole + 2 bags tortilla chips + serving bowl and basket	
Caesar salad and dressing + serving bowl and serving utensils	
Pasta salad + serving dish and serving spoon	
Veggie tray + dip + napkins	
Hummus (2) and pita bread + platter/bowl	
Fruit tray + serving tongs	
Red Solo cups (24) + apples (12) + cutting board and knife	
Paper plates (50) + utensils (plastic forks and knives)	
Frozen strawberries (4 pints) for smoothies + green garbage bags (4)	
Chocolate milk (12 cups/3 L) + bananas (8) (for smoothies)	
Cookies or squares or muffins + serving platter and tongs	
Blender + pitcher (for serving smoothies)	

Go to www.hockeyfood.com for a downloadable copy of this chart.

TEAM POTLUCK SIGN-UP SHEET

Coordinator: Number of people:

Theme: *Meatball Subs and Pasta and Morning Banana Split Smoothies (recipes on www.hockeyfood.com)*

Meal Items	Player & Parent
Frozen cooked meatballs (2 lbs./1 kg) + slow cooker + serving spoon	
Frozen cooked meatballs (2 lbs./1 kg) + slow cooker + serving spoon	
Good-quality tomato sauce (5) + can opener (if needed)	
Cooked pasta + kettle and strainer + slow cooker and serving utensil	
Shredded cheese (2 lbs./1 kg) + serving dish and serving tongs	
Submarine buns (45) + serving basket and serving tongs	
Caesar salad and dressing + serving bowl and serving utensils	
Green salad and dressing + serving bowl and serving utensils	
Veggie tray + dip + napkins	
Hummus (2) + pita bread + platter or bowl	
Fruit tray + serving tongs	
Red Solo cups (24) + apples (12) + cutting board and knife	
Paper plates (50) + utensils (plastic forks and knives)	
Frozen strawberries (4 pints) + serving bowl + green garbage bags (4)	
Chocolate milk (12 cups/3 L) + bananas (8) (for smoothies)	
Cookies or squares or muffins + serving platter and tongs	
Shredded Parmesan cheese (3 cups/750 mL) + napkins	

Go to www.hockeyfood.com for a downloadable copy of this chart.

TEAM POTLUCK SIGN-UP SHEET

Coordinator: Number of people:

Theme: *Stephanie Richardson's Ideal Food Weekend (recipes on www.hockeyfood.com)*

Meal Items	**Player & Parent**
Sliced cooked chicken (2 lbs./1 kg) + slow cooker and serving tongs	
Frozen cooked meatballs (2 lbs./1 kg)	
Cooked whole-wheat penne	
Cooked whole-wheat spaghetti	
Tomato sauce	
Garden salad and dressing + serving bowl and serving utensils	
Caesar salad and dressing + serving bowl and serving utensils	
Pasta salad + serving dish and serving spoon	
Veggie tray + dip + napkins	
Hummus (2) and pita bread + platter or bowl	
Fruit tray + serving tongs	
Cookies + serving platter and serving tongs	
Red Solo cups (24)	
Paper plates (50) + serving utensils (plastic forks and knives)	
Tortilla chips and salsa + bowls and basket	
BYOB (booze and beverages)	

Go to www.hockeyfood.com for a downloadable copy of this chart.

AID: ATHLETIC IMPROVEMENT DRINK

MAKE YOUR OWN!

Player name: _____

AID name: _____

Pre-game or post-game: _____

Ratings: _____

**Start with ½ cup (125 mL) pure coconut water,
then add one ingredient from each column below.**

Liquid (1 to 1½ cups/ 250 to 375 mL)	Sodium (½ tsp/2.5 mL)	Sweetener (½ tsp/2.5 mL)	100% pure fruit juice (max ½ cup/125 mL)
Water	Himalayan salt	Pure maple syrup	Watermelon
Herbal tea		Raw honey	Citrus (orange, lemon, or grapefruit)
		Agave syrup	Pineapple
			Apple
			Pomegranate
			Bloo juice

Tip *If players are undergoing a radical loss of electrolytes, they may experience painful cramping. To help avoid this, add ¼ tsp (1 mL) crushed magnesium tablets or powder to their drink.*

Go to www.hockeyfood.com for a downloadable copy of this chart.

PRE-GAME MEAL

Player name: _____

Pre-game meal name: _____

Ratings: _____

Choose one item from each column below.

Protein (6 oz/175 g)	Carbohydrates (1 to 2 cups/ 250 to 500 mL)	Veggies (Unlimited)	Sauces & Dips (¼ to ½ cup/ 60 to 125 mL)
chicken	brown rice	artichokes	Alfredo sauce
meatballs	white pasta	asparagus	curry sauce
quinoa	multi-grain bread	avocado	Redden's Rippin' Guacamole (page 128)
salmon	quinoa	broccoli	Quick-Hands Hummus (page 123)
tilapia	sweet potatoes	carrots	meat sauce
tuna		cauliflower	pesto
		celery	Heatley's Light the Lamp Salsa (page 131)
		cucumbers	teriyaki sauce
		lettuce	tomato sauce
		onions	Tripping Tzatziki (page 124)
		red pepper	
		tabbouleh	
		tomatoes	
		Winger Green Juice (page 67)	

Go to www.hockeyfood.com for a downloadable copy of this chart.

POST-GAME SNACK

MAKE YOUR OWN!

Player name: _____

Snack name: _____

Ratings: _____

Choose one item from each column below.

Fluids (1 to 2 cups/250 to 500 mL)	Snack Choices (amounts specified)
water	1 Chewy Bar-Down (page 118)
coconut water	3 quinoa crackers and 2 tbsp (30 mL) hummus or natural peanut butter
sports AID (see pages 30–31)	½ to 1 cup (125 to 250 mL) Penalty-Kill Parfaits (page 89)
soy milk	1 to 2 hard-boiled eggs and ½ cup (125 mL) veggie sticks
chocolate milk (see page 33)	¼ to ½ cup (60 to 125 mL) Rink Mix (page 108)
	1 to 2 Power Pucks (page 114)
	handful of almonds or mixed nuts (2 tbsp/30 mL to ¼ cup/60 mL)

Go to www.hockeyfood.com for a downloadable copy of this chart.

SNIPER SMOOTHIE

Player name: _____

Smoothie name: _____

Pre-game or post-game: _____

Ratings: _____

Choose one ingredient from each row below and blend well.   **Amount**

Base liquid	Water (as much as desired)	Coconut water	Milk	Almond milk	Rice milk		1 cup (250 mL)
Supplemental liquid	Orange juice	Cranberry juice	Pome-granate juice	Bloo juice	Ice (as much as desired)		¼ cup (60 mL)
Fruit	Straw-berries	Blue-berries	Banana or kiwi	Pineapple or mango	Apple or apple-sauce	Avocado (one-quarter)	½ cup (125 mL)
Veggie	Kale (centre rib removed, roughly chopped)	Spinach	Baby carrots	Cucumber	Cooked sweet potatoes or pure pumpkin purée	Wheat grass	1 to 2 cups (250 to 500 mL)
Protein boost	Plain Greek yogurt (½ cup/ 125 mL)	Nut butter (1 tbsp/ 15 mL)	Cooked quinoa (¼ cup/ 60 mL)	Protein powder (as per directions to body weight and age)	Frozen green peas		As specified
Sweetener	Pure maple syrup	Raw honey	Agave syrup				Up to 1 tbsp (15 mL)
Flavouring	Ground cinnamon	Ground nutmeg	Dark cocoa powder	Cocoa nibs	Lime juice	Lemon juice	To taste

Go to www.hockeyfood.com for a downloadable copy of this chart.

POWER-PLAY LUNCH BOWL

MAKE YOUR OWN!

Player name: _____

Lunch bowl name: _____

Pre-game or post-game: _____

Ratings: _____

Choose one ingredient from each row below and layer in a serving bowl.

Legume, cooked (drained and rinsed if canned) (¼ cup/60 mL)	Chickpeas	Black beans	Kidney beans	Lentils	
Grain, cooked (½ cup/125 mL)	Barley	Quinoa	Rice	Noodles	Bench-Clearing Bean Dip (page 132)
Protein, cooked (4–6 oz/110–175 g)	Chicken	Shellfish	Tofu (firm)	Beef or pork	Shredded cheese 1 oz (30 g)
Leafy greens (unlimited)	Arugula	Spinach	Romaine lettuce	Mesclun mix	Iceberg lettuce
Veggies (unlimited)	Carrots, grated	Green onions, minced	Broccoli florets, fresh or frozen	Peas or corn, fresh or frozen	Sweet peppers (red, yellow, orange, or green), diced
Dressing	Big Rig Ranch (page 149) (1 tbsp/15 mL)	Clutch Caesar (page 146) (1 tbsp/15 mL)	Balsamic Winger-grette (page 150) (1 tbsp/15 mL)	Visor-Foggin' Asian Dressing (page 153) (1 tbsp/15 mL)	Heatley's Light the Lamp Salsa (page 131) (¼ cup/60 mL)
Add-ons	Avocado (one-quarter)	Bacon, crumbled (1 tbsp/15 mL)	Dried unsweetened raisins, blueberries, cranberries (1 tbsp/15 mL)	Pumpkin or sunflower seeds, raw unsalted (2 tbsp/30 mL)	

Go to www.hockeyfood.com for a downloadable copy of this chart.

SOUP

Player name: _____

Soup name: _____

Pre-game or post-game: _____

Ratings: _____

Combine one ingredient from each row below in a saucepan and heat through.

Liquid (2 cups/500 mL)	Beef broth (reduced-sodium)	Chicken broth (reduced-sodium)	Vegetable broth (reduced-sodium)	Tomato juice (reduced-sodium)	¼ cup (60 mL) lite coconut milk diluted with water to equal 2 cups (500 mL)
Veggies (1 cup/250 mL)	Tomatoes, diced	Sweet peppers, carrots, or celery, chopped	Broccoli florets, fresh or frozen	Baby spinach leaves	Peas or corn, frozen
Carb (¼ cup/60 mL)	Quinoa, cooked	Pasta, cooked	Black beans (rinsed and drained if canned)	Rice noodles, cooked	Barley, cooked
Protein (2 oz/60 g)	Beef, cooked	Shrimp, cooked	Quinoa, cooked	Tofu (firm)	Chicken, cooked
Seasoning (to taste)	Fresh herbs (basil, parsley, cilantro), chopped				

About the Authors

Canadian food media spokesperson Korey Kealey, co-founder of www.enerjive.com, has teamed up with celebrity pro hockey wife and nutritionist Erin Phillips to bring you The Ultimate Cookbook for Hockey Families, *a bible for hockey parents looking to fuel their players for optimal health and endurance.*

Erin is not only the main chef for hockey star Chris Phillips and a recreational hockey player herself, but she is also a hockey mom. Having three very active children (Ben 11, Zoë 10, and Niomi 7) requires her to stay on top of meal planning and hydration so her kids can stay at the top of their game. Erin is passionate about sharing an easier approach to feeding kids on the go to enhance their happiness and hockey performance.

After studying human kinetics at the University of Ottawa, Erin continued her education at the Canadian School of Natural Nutrition, where she found her true passion as a registered nutritional consulting practitioner (RNCP), specializing in sports nutrition. Today, Erin is devoted to demystifying the nutritional and hydration needs of hockey kids and figure skaters everywhere.

As the founder of Kitchen Konnected, Korey's natural talent for food styling and media communications is put to good use working with such names as Foodland Ontario, Ontario Egg Farmers, Crock Pot, Oster, and Jarden Consumer Solution. Being knee-deep in the kitchen developing healthy recipes is a dream come true for Korey, and nothing makes her happier than sharing her favourite entertaining tips along with her culinary creations. Korey has worked in all facets of the food industry, and as co-founder of enerjive inc., she has proven her commitment to designing foods that fully support energy and health.

After completing her Bachelor of Arts at the University of Ottawa, Korey followed her passion for nutrition at the University of Guelph by completing her food and nutrition management diploma. Since then, Korey hasn't looked back, and enjoys sharing her "cheater" recipes as well as cooking tips with other parents who, like her, may be crunched for time.

With Korey's husband, Liam, and her three kids (Alexander 17, Adam 15, and Rebecca 11) and their demanding competitive hockey schedules, she often lives at the arena and knows how challenging it can be to serve nutritious meals in between ice time, which is why she is so passionate about teamwork. Using Korey's simple solutions, the whole family will be playing together in the kitchen without a single misconduct in no time!

Acknowledgments

Erin would like to thank...

Korey Kealey, for turning this dream into a reality. Your knowledge, skills, and professionalism are truly admirable. I have learned a lot from you, and I am truly grateful for our friendship.

Chris, my very patient and amazing husband, for guiding us on our journey with endless amounts of support, advice, and inspiration to see this project through. This would have never materialized without you. I love you.

Our children, Ben, Zöe, and Niomi, for your inspiration to write this book, your dedication to your sports, and for being the official taste testers … lots of love.

My mom, Sherline, and my dad, Barry, for living and promoting a healthy way of life, serving delicious meals, and keeping expectations high!

My sister, Kristina, for being a great hockey mom and providing us with feedback and great advice.

The Usher and Brown families, for your friendship, support, and coming to the rescue with cell phones in DR.

All of our hockey buds, for providing their great recipes and tips and family traditions, and their moms/wives/girlfriends, for opening their kitchens and giving us a glimpse of everyday life.

My figure skating buds, for the great recipes and friendship and support.

Aaron Robinson and the Senators organization, for supporting this project as well as Chris and me throughout the years.

The team at Big Rig, for recipe ideas and being the best place to have our cookbook meetings!

Korey would like to thank...

Erin Phillips, for your cheery early morning calls! It has been a pleasure to work with you on this brilliant idea of yours. How could I say no? I'm glad I didn't. Your energy and passion for family, sport, and nutrition is a gift and so are you.

Liam, my mentor, challenger, and best friend. You always have my back and I love you for it and for being the most dedicated hockey dad I know.

Our kids, Alexander, Adam, and Rebecca, the hockey players I love to feed and who have made the past 12 years in arenas fun and exciting.

My mom, Estelle, for being such a talented foodie and exposing me to only yummy real foods.

My dad, Doug Twohey, for being a creative and resourceful businessman and sharing his ideas with me.

Elva Kealey, friend, mother-in-law, and the backbone supporter of our family! You are a rink runner, cheerleader, meal maker, and an amazing gramma!

Kelly White, my sister, for editing, reviewing, commenting, and supporting me in all of my adventures and being my biggest cheerleader in a quiet way.

Krista Kealey, my friend and sister-in-law, for being a tireless supporter, promoter, and brainstormer.

Rebecca Hollingsworth, for fabulous marketing ideas, for listening, for dropping everything to take photos, and for being an incredible friend.

Erin and Korey would like to thank...

Tracy Bordian, our incredibly multitalented, organized, insightful, determined, and patient editor. What can we say? You took us on with possibly the tightest deadline ever known to the publishing world, and we feel blessed and thankful for you (even when you were annoyed with us)! You are a treasure.

Kyle Gell, for the interior design and seeing our vision even when we couldn't.

Miriam Blier, for the fantastic cover design.

Val Keeler and assistant Caitlin from Valberg Imaging, for your gorgeous photos, flexibility, and quick turnaround with edits and changes. It was so much fun during our photo shoots!

Laurie Brown, for the nutritional evaluation on every recipe.

Shari Canning, for our early-day editing (you and Tracy could connect and share stories).

Kathy Smart, for sharing self-publishing intelligence and every resource requested, as well as your gluten-free contribution to our book.

Janet Podleski, for great advice on not self-publishing.

Michelle Bailey, for having our backs and keeping us organized at every turn.

Brendon Peterson, for having faith in our vision.

Sarah Scott, our publisher, for her expertise in managing the many components of getting this book onto shelves across Canada.

Roger Deveau and Sarah Roberts, our web designers, for your enthusiasm and efficient translation of materials to web. www.hockeyfood.com was a great find, and we look forward to the next part of this project online.

The parents of our kids' hockey teams, for being guinea pigs for our potluck shenanigans and showing us that it really works even when you thought it would fail.

Lianne Laing, for your friendship and eternal support and faith in us.

Melissa Lamb, for your hockey connections and support.

Alexa Spas, for being our foodie friend.

Progressive supplements, for making delicious supplements that support the body in everyday life and sport. We are happy to share some of your products with hockey families.

Lagostina, for supplying us with the best cookware and kitchen gear. Having reliable yet affordable equipment can be half the battle in the kitchen.

enerjive, for the fabulous-tasting and nutrient-dense quinoa crackers that kept us full and happy as we slaved on this book. There is nothing else like them.

The Recipes

Photo Credits

Personal photographs of players and families are reproduced with permission and are copyright respective players and families.

All other photographs by Valerie Keeler/Valberg Images and copyright © Erin Phillips and Korey Kealey, with the exception of the following:

p. v   © iStock.com/fotofermer

p. ix   © iStock.com/Alina555

p. x   © iStock.com/kativ

pp. 12–13   © Volkova Irina/Shutterstock.com

p. 17   © iStock.com/gilaxia

p. 18   © iStock.com/mauhorng

p. 19   © iStock.com/fuzzbones0

p. 20   © iStock.com/galaiko

p. 22   © iStock.com/ermingut

p. 23   © iStock.com/celsopupo

p. 26   © bigjohn36/Thinkstock

p. 28   © iStock.com/lostbear

p. 29   © iStock.com/adamkaz

p. 33   © iStock.com/bhofack2

p. 34   © Ryan McVay/Photodisc/Thinkstock

pp. 36–37   © iStock.com/Vanell

p. 38   © iStock.com/gilaxia

pp. 39, 46   (clipboard) © Mega Pixel/Shutterstock.com

p. 40   © iStock.com/Juanmonino

p. 41   © iStock.com/princessdlaf

p. 49   © iStock.com/bigjohn36

pp. 52–53   © Shooter Bob Square Lenses/Shutterstock.com

p. 54   © iStock.com/aluxum

p. 55   © iStock.com/Natikka

p. 56   (cucumber) © iStock.com/SednevaAnna

p. 56   (coloured peppers) © iStock.com/AlexMax

p. 57   © iStock.com/bonchan

pp. 58–59   © iStock.com/BanksPhotos

p. 62   (Erik Karlsson) © Matt Zambonin/Freestyle Photography/OSHC

p. 71   © iStock.com/StockPhotosArt

p. 72   © iStock.com/VeselovaElena

p. 79   © iStock.com/MSPhotographic

p. 85   © iStock.com/letty17

p. 98   © iStock.com/ineskoleva

p. 107   © iStock.com/Kasiam

p. 110   © iStock.com/ReyKamensky

p. 141   © iStock.com/DNY59

p. 172   (Kathy Smart) © Jennifer Wood

p. 176   © iStock.com/MargoeEdwards

p. 190   © iStock.com/AlasdairJames

p. 212   © iStock.com/Floortje

p. 227   (Tessa Virtue) © Myra Klarman

p. 234   © iStock.com/Elenathewise

p. 254   © iStock.com/doram

pp. 268–269   © iStock.com/REKINC1980

p. 271   © iStock.com/aksphoto